FROM RADICAL EMPIRICISM
TO ABSOLUTE IDEALISM

JUSTUS HARTNACK

STUDIES IN THE HISTORY OF PHILOSOPHY

VOLUME 1

The Edwin Mellen Press
Lewiston/Queenston

B
802
.H28
1987

Library of Congress Cataloging-in-Publication Date

Hartnack, Justus.
  From radical empiricism to absolute idealism.

  (Studies in the history of philosophy; v. 1)
  Bibliography: p.
  Includes index.
  1. Philosophy, Modern--18th century. 2. Philosophy, Modern--19th
century. I. Title. II. Series: Studies in the history of philosophy (Lewiston,
N.Y.); v. 1.
  B802.H28 1986   190   86-8603
  ISBN 0-88946-304-2

This is volume 1 in the continuing series
Studies in the History of Philosophy
Volume 1 ISBN 0-88946-304-2
SHP Series ISBN 0-88946-300-X

The Edwin Mellen Press   The Edwin Mellen Press
Box 450   Box 67
Lewiston, New York   Queenston, Ontario
USA   14092   CANADA   LOS 1LO

Printed in the United States of America

BOOKS BY JUSTUS HARTNACK

ANALYSIS OF THE PROBLEM OF PERCEPTION IN BRITISH
EMPIRICISM

PHILOSOPHICAL PROBLEMS, A Modern Introduction

FILOSOFISKE ESSAYS

WITTGENSTEIN AND MODERN PHILOSOPHY

DEN YDRE VERDENS EKSISTENS

FILOSOFISKE PROBLEMER OG FILOSOFISKE
ARGUMENTATIONER

KANT'S EPISTEMOLOGY

POLITIK OG FILOSOFI

KANT

HISTORY OF PHILOSOPHY

LANGUAGE AND PHILOSOPHY

MENNESKERETTIGHEDER

CONTENTS

I   **Introduction**   *1*

II   **David Hume**   *11*
The Impossibility of Radical Empiricism

III   **Kantianism** *as a Decisive Step towards*   *21*
Absolute Idealism

IV   **Fichte**   *35*
The First but Decisive Step of Absolute
Idealism

V   **Schelling**   *67*

VI   **Hegel**
    1.   *The Preface*   *89*
    2.   *Introduction*   *106*
    3.   *Sense-Certainty*   *109*
    4.   *Perception*   *117*
    5.   *Understanding*   *123*
    6.   *Self-Consciousness*
        a.   *Lordship and Bondage*   *141*
        b.   *The Unhappy Consciousness*   *160*

VII   **Concluding Remarks**   *167*

VIII   **Short Biographies**
    1.   *David Hume*   *173*
    2.   *Immanuel Kant*   *176*
    3.   *Johann Gottlieb Fichte*   *180*
    4.   *Friedrich Schelling*   *184*
    5.   *Georg Wilhelm Friedrich Hegel*   *190*

IX   **Notes**   *197*

X   **Index**   *211*

FROM RADICAL EMPIRICISM TO ABSOLUTE IDEALISM

Introduction

The advance of human thought, be it within the natural sciences or within philosophy, does not proceed as a continuous movement. The development is not like the growth of a plant which occurs, so to speak, along a straight line and without interruptions. Instead it is a development which takes place in leaps, and, at least so far as philosophy is concerned, in dialectical leaps. It is when human thought in its dialectical development has reached a fundamental impasse or has arrived at fundamentally conflicting views that the philosophic situation is ripe for a new, often revolutionary, metaphysical or conceptual system. The closer the conflict is to the very root of thought itself the greater the philosophic creativity and ingenuity it requires in order to overcome it.

Already in pre-Socratic philosophy such a deep and fundamental conflict was arrived at. Against Heraclitus' dictum or thesis that whatever is (Being) is in a constant flux - nothing remains unchanged in two consecutive moments - we have Parmenides' antithesis that whatever is must be unchangeable. It was this philosophic crisis which gave rise to the metaphysical systems of Plato and Aristotle.

A different but equally deep and fundamental metaphysical or conceptual crisis came to the fore in the 18th century. In 1739 David Hume published his **Treatise on Human Nature**, a work which became the classical work of radical empiricism. It was, and still is, generally regarded as a work which has delivered a decisive blow to classical rationalism.

Radical empiricism cannot be upheld either. Since it shall be examined in the following chapter, it will here suffice to mention only the following. Radical empiricism admits into the realm of existence only perceptions, and holds that the function of words is to name perceptions. From this it follows that it cannot legitimize words like 'I' or 'object' (in the same sense in which these words have another logical status than the words naming the properties of the object). Such words have therefore, in Hume's words, to be committed to the flames. But as I shall try to show in the next chapter, a language deprived of such words cannot fulfill its function as a language. Radical empiricism is consequently a false philosophy.

With neither classical rationalism nor radical empiricism as tenable philosophies a new metaphysical system was needed. This new metaphysics saw its beginning in 1781, i.e. the year Kant published his **Kritik der reinen Vernunft**, and was completed in 1807 when Hegel's **Phänomenologie des Geistes** appeared. These 26 years from 1781 to 1807 were the years in which German or Absolute Idealism was born. It is these twenty-six years the following pages shall portray. It is probably no exaggeration to say that during this period, during these mere twenty-six years, philosophy, with enormous inertia and acceleration, whirled toward its metaphysical culmination. To many an ear it may sound provoking to maintain that what forcefully and with all the power of a genius began with Kant and was brought to its highest fulfillment with Hegel - a fulfillment, however, which in many respects was not a perfection but a rejection of Kantianism - represents one of the greatest break-throughs in the history of philosophic thought. Provoking or not, it is nevertheless what I shall try to show.

The fact that metaphysical thinking through absolute idealism reached a peak does not imply that it necessarily represents the truth. But whether or not it does so, it does represent a philosophic thinking not only of great interest but also of the greatest importance. It is of importance because the problem it tries to solve is a problem which is both fundamental and inevitable.

The problem is this. To know, to be capable of acquiring knowledge, implies among other things the following two things. It implies that there is a knowing subject, i.e. a consciousness capable of thinking and acquiring knowledge; that there is an 'I' or an 'Ego.' It also implies that there is something one acquires knowledge about; that there is something which constitutes the object of knowledge. To acquire knowledge thus involves a relation between a knowing subject and a known object. That this relation necessarily carries with it a problem, is not difficult to see. If one knows something one then knows that something or other is the case. One knows some facts. And since to know a fact involves concepts which in turn involves a language it follows that to know something implies that one is able to express it in a language. The relation between the knowing subject and the known object thus is a relation between language and that which language is about. According to our ordinary pre-philosophic view, that which language is about, the object of language, has ontological priority, and language which describes the object of language is secondary. One does not begin by having a language and then, as a second step, searches for something to which the language can be applied. It must, so it seems, be the other way around. There is a world to describe; and it is because there is a world to describe that language has developed.

This view of the relation between language and that which language is about was the view held by Hume. Perceptions exist prior to the names of these perceptions. In the naming relation the name presupposes that which the name is naming. As already mentioned, Hume's view implied the impossibility of language and therefore also the impossibility of knowledge.

In order to rescue knowledge from Hume's deadly attack Kant revolutionized philosophy; he revolutionized the ordinary view of the relation between language and the object of language. Kant's view (which shall be described later) was that nothing can be known unless it is by help of concepts; and since concepts are subjective conditions of knowledge it follows that the object of knowledge is determined by these concepts and consequently by the subject. Or to express it differently, since the concepts are necessary conditions of language the object of language is determined by the concept of language. It is one of Kant's greatest contributions to philosophy to have made clear and to have emphasized the fundamental significance and the necessary function of language for all knowledge and experience.

However important Kantianism was, and is, it is nevertheless pregnant with a fatal defect. Because even though Kant was right in emphasizing that concepts - and therefore also language - are necessary conditions for knowledge, his system did involve an unbridgeable gulf between the object as it appears when it is conceived by help of the concepts and the object these concepts are applied to, i.e. the object as it is when it is not involved in the cognitive process, or, as Kant expresses it, "in itself." The object in itself, the object to which the concepts are applied, is not only thought of as an object different from the object as it appears when it is conceived by help of the concepts; it is in fact a concept of an object in danger of being not just an unknown object - an object of which nothing whatever can be said - but of being a meaningless concept.

The concept of the thing in itself is, and by post-Kantian philosophy was, regarded as a fatal defect. The aim of post-

Kantian philosophy was, consequently, to change that philosophy to such an extent that the defect was eliminated without thereby eliminating what was regarded as the true element in the Kantian philosophy. The aim, in other words, was to avoid that the Kantian insight that concepts, and therefore also language, constitute necessary conditions for knowledge should entail dualism.

But when the first of the great post-Kantian philosophers, Johann Gottlieb Fichte, made such an attempt, Kant publicly denounced it. However, Fichte's philosophic system is the first formulation of German or absolute idealism. It was a system which Schelling and Hegel, each in their own way, modified, changed and, at least according to themselves, improved, not to say completed.

Without getting into details - in a later chapter Fichte's philosophy shall be examined more closely - it suffices to say that if the above mentioned dualism (the view that there is a radical and unbridgeable gulf between subject and object) had to be avoided - and this is what absolute idealism is all about - it seems unavoidable to identify subject and object. Such an identification was precisely what Fichte attempted to undertake.

The problem about the relation between subject and object - a problem which, as just described, is central to German and absolute idealism - is a problem which is implicit in the nature of knowledge itself. It is implicit in the very concept of knowledge. A necessary presupposition for the application of the concept of knowledge is that there is a knowing subject and that there is something which the knowing subject knows, i.e. that there is an object of knowledge.

What makes absolute idealism not only interesting but also, as already mentioned, important is that the views concerning the relationships between subject and object held by philosophers from Hume to Hegel exhaust the logically possible views and that the views held by the absolute idealists are the only possible alternatives if one regards as erroneous the views of Hume and Kant. And since, as I shall argue, the views of Hume and Kant, each in their own and different ways, are untenable, it follows that absolute idealism is in fact the only remaining possibility.

As stated above, the problem of the relation between subject and object can be conceived of as a relation between language and that which language is about, i.e. between language and the object of language. As I have just maintained, the only three possibilities of conceiving of this relation correspond to the three views held by respectively Hume, Kant, and absolute idealism. These three possibilities are the following. (1) Language is about a non-linguistic reality. A language which is not a language about something is not a language at all. And although a language may be a meta-language, i.e. may be a language about another language which in turn may itself be a language about yet another language, the series 'a language which is about a language which is about a language ...' cannot be an infinite series. It must necessarily be the case that there is a language which is not about another language but is about a non-linguistic reality. (2) Language is about a non-linguistic reality. But the non-linguistic reality language is about is in itself something utterly unknown. Since we conceive, understand and comprehend only by applying concepts and since concepts have sense only in connection with a language, it follows that the non-linguistic reality cannot in itself, i.e. independently of the concepts and language applied to it, be comprehended or constitute an object of thought. It is totally ineffable. (3) According to the third possibility the concept of a non-linguistic reality is in fact itself a linguistic concept. It is a concept which is embedded in the very concept of language. The concept of a non-linguistic reality is entailed by the concept of language. In other words, a necessary condition of giving a meaning to the concept of a non-linguistic reality is that it is negated: it is only by understanding this dialectic element involved in the concept of language, namely, that language by logical necessity is connected with the concept of a non-linguistic reality and that this reality therefore cannot be separate from and be independent of the language which is its logical home.

The view expressed in (3) corresponds to the view held by absolute idealism. To be sure, absolute idealism does not express itself in these idioms. It does not express itself in terms of language but by more metaphysically and ontologically sounding concepts - concepts such as 'the absolute,' 'the I,' 'the non-I,' etc. The logical nature of the problem, however, its immense complexity and its unavoidability as well as its importance are the same. That is, its unavoidability, its importance and its extreme difficulty remain the same whether the problem is formulated in its classical way or is formulated in terms of language. This does not mean, however, that the two formulations are equally accepted. This they are not. To formulate the problem in terms of language is a result of a philosophical classification of the metaphysical and ontological terms used in the classical formulation. To view the problem as a problem about the relation between language and that which language is about is therefore to view the problem from a philosophically more advanced perspective than to view it from the classical point of view.

But since the problem is, as just emphasized, fundamental and unavoidable it is natural, not to say necessary, that it

constituted the main problem of philosophy at a time in which
metaphysical thinking displayed its greatest quality, energy and
concentration.

Since Hume's concept of the relation between language and
that which language is about leads, as I shall try to show, to a
negation of the very language used to formulate the problem only
Kantianism and absolute idealism remains. Kantianism, however,
entails the contradictory, or even meaningless concept of the
thing in itself. Kantianism as such must therefore be rejected.
However difficult it would be to accept, philosophy consequently
seems conceptually forced to maintain that, stated in classical
metaphysical terms, the object of consciousness, in the world
which constitutes the object of knowledge for consciousness or
the I, and therefore is identical with what German idealism termed
the non-I or the non-Ego, in the last analysis not only is
conceptually determined but also is of a conceptual nature.
Stated in terms, not of consciousness and its object or of the I
and the non-I, but of language and that which language is about,
it turns out that the thesis of German idealism is not only not
difficult to accept but seems in fact to be a view which it is
necessary to hold.

In the following pages I shall try, first of all, to examine
the problem in its historical development and the dialectical
movement of the concepts such as it is expressed by the
philosophers described.   Next, I shall attempt to translate the
problem into a problem of language and its object concluding by
giving a formulation of absolute idealism in such terms.

One may accept or reject Absolute Idealism. However, if one
rejects it, it means, according to the view expressed in the
preceeding pages, that one by necessity accepts either
Kantianism or Radical Empiricism; not to do so would mean to be

philosophically indifferent to a problem which philosophy, and therefore human reason, cannot escape. It is a problem which is at the root of thought itself. It is, so to speak, the metaphysical problem **par excellence.**

David Hume

The Impossibility of Radical Empiricism

David Hume's philosophy is of importance for, among other reasons, the following ones. First of all, he was able to formulate an extreme or a radical form for empiricism and to draw out the philosophical consequences of such a view. This in itself is a historical contribution. Because when the philosophic consequences of the premises of radical empiricism are drawn it is seen that it is a self-negating system. Secondly, his philosophy is important because it represents the one pole of the spectrum whose other pole is absolute idealism. The movement from radical empiricism to absolute idealism represents not only the movement from one pole to another; it also represents the spectrum which, with respect to the problem of the relation between language and its object, constitutes the only possibility. Not without some justification, although not without some simplification either, it may be maintained that without a Hume there would be no Kant, and without a Kant neither a Fichte, a Schelling, nor a Hegel.

Let us examine Hume's premises. To observe, to have sensations of different kinds is to receive sense-impressions. Most sense-impressions are what he calls complex impressions. To see an apple is to be presented with a complex impression. It is a complex of the red and yellow color of the apple; it possesses a special shape, a special taste, and several other such so-called simple impressions. All these different simple impressions constitute what we call an apple. Hume's first premise is accordingly this: To maintain that something exists is to say that a certain sense-impression, simple or complex, appears or, under special circumstances, will appear. His second premise concerns the relation between language and that which language is about, or in other words, the relation between language and the actually or potentially appearing sense-impressions.

According to the Humean philosophy words are names of sense-impressions. Essential in this connection is that language is conceived as secondary in its relationship to the sense-impressions it is naming. Sense-impressions exist independently of the words naming them; they exist ready-made to be named. The world of things and facts exists prior to and independent of language. To maintain that a sense-impression exists or appears ready-made to be named is the same as to maintain, what is untenable, that a sense-impression can be conceived, identified, and re-identified as this or that sense-impression quite independently of language.

Corresponding to the second premise is a third premise. In order that a word is meaningful it must be a name either of a simple impression or of a complex impression. If it does not satisfy this condition the word is void of meaning; it ought, therefore, as Hume expresses it, to "be committed to the flames."

Hume's radical empiricism is thus determined by the following three theories: (1) A theory about existence, the theory namely, that whatever exists must appear or must be able to appear as a, simple or complex, impression; (2) a theory about the relation between language and the non-linguistic reality language is used about, the theory, namely, that language in its existence is posterior to the non-linguistic reality. Language presupposes that this reality already is conceived and comprehended; and, finally, (3) a theory about the meaning of words, the theory, namely, that a word has meaning only if it is a name of a sense-impression.

According to this kind of radical empiricism quite a few words ought to be committed to the flames. What is fatal, however, is that also words which are necessary conditions for having any language at all must be committed to the flames. In what follows I shall concentrate on only two such words: the word 'thing' and the word 'I'.

An apple is an object, a thing. The word 'apple' has meaning, according to Hume, because it refers to or names a complex impression. It is a complex impression which can be analyzed in terms of the simple impressions making up the complex impression.

A conjunction of all the names of the simple impressions exhausts the meaning of the term 'apple.' It could, on Hume's premises, mean nothing over and above such a conjunction.

Hume, however, failed to make an important distinction, a failure he shares with most of the classical phenomenalists, Berkeley in particular, the distinction, namely, between the ontological and the epistemological aspects of the problem. The ontological problem is the problem of what constitutes a physical object, e.g. an apple, whereas the epistemological problem is the problem of how the existence of a physical object such as an apple is verified. The answer to the epistemological question is of course that one verifies the existence of a particular object in terms of the different available sense-impressions. Whether this particular object is an apple is determined by ascertaining whether it has the appropriate sense-impressions, that is, whether it tastes, smells, and looks as an apple is supposed to taste, smell and to look. It would be absurd, however, to maintain that an apple consists of or is constituted by a combination of a certain taste, smell and appearance. An apple has or possesses a certain taste but it does not consist of it. Hume's failure to make the distinction is necessitated by his theories of existence and of meaning. If a word has meaning only as a name of sense-impressions, and nothing but sense-impressions can meaningfully be said to have existence, he is bound to assert that an object can consist of nothing but sense-impressions.

Furthermore, to maintain that an object consists of nothing over and above sense-impressions makes it impossible to have a language. The logic of the concept of an object and the logic of the concept of a sense-impression are different and only unsolvable puzzles result if the two concepts are treated without doing justice to those differences. The use of language requires that we use the concept of an object or a thing. It does not make sense to talk about a sense-impression (or if one prefers a sense-datum) lying on the top of the table or that I put it in my pocket. Words naming sense-impressions or sense-data are by their very logic conceived as words naming properties of an object or a thing. I do not hold a color in my hand; I hold a colored object in my hand. A smell and a taste are by necessity a smell and a taste of something. Furthermore, a simple sense-impression is a universal. The red color and the sweet taste, or if one prefers, the redness in the red color and the sweetness in the sweet taste are universals. Names of simple sense-impressions lose their meaning if they cannot serve as predicates of things and objects. It follows, therefore, that an object or a thing is a combination of simple sense-impressions. It has no meaning to say that a simple sense-impression can be a property of another simple sense-impression or of a combination of simple sense-impressions. An object or a thing, however, is a paradigm

---

of an individual. Whereas a simple sense-impression is that which by necessity is a property of an object, an object cannot meaningfully be said to be a property neither of a sense-impression nor of another object.

It is, moreover, the case that a condition for having a language is that what is talked about can be identified and re-identified. The chair I am sitting in is the same chair in which I was sitting yesterday. I recognize it as being the same chair by its color, its shape, etc. The car I am driving is the very same car I bought some years back. I recognize it as being that specific car by its looks and, in case of doubt, by its license plate. But such things (colors, shapes, license plates, etc.) cannot constitute the final criterion. There could be a chair which is exactly like the chair I take to be my chair; and there could be a car which is exactly like my car, even the license plate is no conclusive proof. It might be the case that somebody had stolen my license plate and put it on the other car. The final criterion must be space-time coordinates of the object. The tree, the house, and the plants are identified and re-identified as being this particular tree, this particular house, and these particular plants because they occupy this particular slice of space at this particular time. But a red color and a sweet taste possess in themselves no individuality. They cannot even individualize the objects of which they are properties.

As already Aristotle argued, the concept of change necessitates the concept of that which remains the same during the change. And Descartes, arguing the same point, illustrated the necessity of the concept of substance by heating a piece of wax which therefore was subjected to a Heraclitian world of flux; and, obviously, language would be impossible if we could not refer to these constantly changing properties as being properties of something which remains identically the same thing during the

process of change. That 'something' is that which is referred to
in the sentence: "This piece of wax is undergoing a process
during which all its properties are constantly changing."[1]

Another word Hume insisted should be committed to the
flames is the word 'I'. Since there possibly cannot be a sense-
impression which the word refers to it must, on Hume's premises,
be a meaningless word. Hume seems to suggest that it is an
empirical fact that no such sense-impression exists. It is as if he
had tried, but tried in vain, to find one. But this would, of
course, have been a futile and even absurd undertaking for at
least two reasons. One reason is this. Whatever sense-
impression Hume, or anybody else, would have it could be known,
a priori, that it could never qualify as a sense-impression of an
I. Which color should it be? None of course; which kind of
taste? It would be absurd even to suggest that it should have
any taste. The battle would a priori be lost. But even if
somebody, despite the just mentioned argument, should maintain
that he had found a sense impression which could qualify as a
sense-impression of an I it would be a self-refuting proposition.
The fact that it is a sense-impression **he** has entails that he must
be able to claim that it is **his** sense impression. Which again
entails that the 'I' which has the sense-impression of the alleged I
cannot itself be one of his sense impressions. Since sense
impressions do not exist independently of an 'I' which has them,
it follows that it is conceptually impossible to have a sense
impression of an I.

It is also a conceptual impossibility to identify the I with an
entity, e.g. a soul. Two different persons can both identify
themselves by help of the word I. Each of them can use the
expression 'my soul' in the same sense of the word 'my' in which
it is used in expressions such as 'my leg' or 'my stomach.' The
soul which is mine must be numerically different from the soul

which is the soul of another person. If I use the expression 'my soul' (which is a meaningful expression independent of whether there are such things as souls) the word 'my' cannot, of course, refer to the soul. Expressed differently, the term 'I' can be defined neither in physical terms (i.e., in terms of my body) nor in psychological terms – independent of whether the terms are referring to special psychological phenomena or to an alleged soul. Of special interest are the psychological terms classified under the concept of memory. The 17th century British philosopher, John Locke, defined personal identity, i.e. that which constitutes the I and which remains the same from birth to death, in terms of memory. Admittedly, whenever a person makes a memory statement, or a statement which involves memory, the identity of the I is entailed. If I say: "I met him yesterday" the 'I' who met the person referred to by the word 'him' is by necessity the same 'I' who is making the statement now. But this does not entail that the 'I' can be defined in terms of memory. If it did, it would mean that memory enjoyed logical priority over the I in somewhat the same sense in which e.g. hydrogen and oxygen have logical priority over water. The existence of water presupposes the existence of hydrogen and oxygen in the same sense in which, according to Locke's theory, the I presupposes memory. It is easy to see, however, that the converse is the case. It is memory which presupposes the existence of an I which remains one and the same I. It is not memory which enjoys logical priority over the I but the I which enjoys logical priority over memory. Suppose I say that I remember my first schoolday. I can remember some of the teachers, some of the instructions given, and a few other things. It would be absurd, however, if I also maintained that I could remember that it was me. It would be absurd precisely because memory presupposes that I am identically the same I. And that which constitutes a presupposition for memory cannot itself be remembered.[2]

Since memory is a condition for consciousness - is a condition for the unity of consciousness without which there would be no consciousness (a point, we shall see shortly, was argued by Kant) - and the identity of the I is a condition of memory, it follows that this identity, and therefore also the I, is a condition of consciousness. Which is the same as to say that the I is a condition of language.

It is fatal, therefore, to any language to declare, as Hume was bound to, that the word I is a meaningless word. No language can be without a word corresponding to the concept of an I. Just as necessary as it is that a psychological verb has an intentional object, i.e. that which I am thinking of, doubting, believeing in, etc., just as necessary is it that there is an object. There must be a thinker, a doubter, and a believer. For every existing sense impression there must be a person who can say: "I have this particular sense impression." The thinking, the doubting or believing person, i.e. the subject of consciousness, identifies himself by the use of the term 'I.' And since neither a proper name nor a description (description in Russell's sense) can exhaust the meaning of the term 'I' it follows that it cannot be translated without remainder into other terms.[3] It is both a non-empirical and a necessary word.

The concept of the 'I' and the concept of the consciousness and therefore also the concept of language are conceptually inseparable. To maintain that there is a consciousness without a subject is to maintain a conceptual impossibility, and to maintain that there could be a language without the concept of an I built into it is therefore to maintain something equally absurd.

It is of course true that the word 'I' does not require to be used. Children quite often acquire a sufficient command of a language without necessarily having learned the use of the word 'I.' The point is, however, that the concept of the 'I' is a necessity. It is implicit in the concept of sense impression and in the concept of consciousness. It is also implicit in the concept of a language. It follows already from the fact that the use of a language, i.e. the performance of speech acts, is an act of consciousness and that consciousness presupposes the concept of an 'I.'

Although Hume's radical empiricism was destined to collapse it nevertheless had great virtues. After Hume, it took great philosophical courage to assume that sense impressions (such as the red color or the sweet taste) are properties of an object which in itself were supposed to be a special existing thing or object, a thing or an object which in itself, therefore, was different from the properties which were properties of it. Its existence would remain a mystery. It could be neither observed (what is observable are sense impressions) nor described (words used to describe something are names of sense impressions). The problem Hume, in this respect, left for metaphysics (or ontology) to solve thus is this. On the one hand the concept of something which is the bearer of the properties of an object seems a concept which language cannot be without; on the other hand, however, such a concept seems impossible to give any meaning. The solution must be, therefore, to preserve the concept but preserve it as a concept that does not have as a function to be a name of or to refer to anything. It is a necessary condition of language but it is not an ontological word.

Hume also deserves credit for having argued persuasively that the word 'I' cannot be an ontological word. In the post-Humean philosophic world few philosophers, if any, would maintain that the word 'I' refers to a special entity, be it a soul, a brain process, or 'my' body as such. Nevertheless, the word cannot be regarded as meaningless since it is a necessary condition of language. The word has a necessary function which it was for Hume's Continental successors to clarify.

Hume's place in the dialectical development of philosophic systems may be, at least from one point of view, that it demonstrated the impossibility of radical empiricism. The demonstration, which surely was not what Hume intended since he advocated such an empiricism, had the form of a transcendental argument. We do in fact have a language (consciousness, experience). From this it follows that the necessary conditions (the categories) for having a language are satisfied. According to its logical structure the transcendental argument is of a negative form. It invalidates and demolishes. The most famous execution of the transcendental argument was Kant's transcendental deduction of the categories in his famous **Critique of Pure Reason.** Also Kant's transcendental deduction is demonstrating by way of the negative. He attempts to prove the validity of the categories by showing the impossibility of having the experience we do have without them.

The impossibility and collapse of radical empiricism necessitated a new philosophic system. It had to be a system which preserved the insight of Hume's philosophy which was regarded as correct, the insight, namely, that words such as 'I' and 'the thing in itself' could not be regarded as ontological words, i.e. could not be regarded as referring to substances; but it also had to be a system which negated what was regarded as Hume's mistake, the mistake, namely, that such words therefore were meaningless. Hume's place in the history of philosophy can therefore, among other things, be seen as a steppingstone, via Kantianism, for absolute idealism.

Kantianism As a Decisive Step Towards Absolute Idealism

One of the essential differences between Hume and Kant is their respective views of the relation between language and that which language is about. To Hume, language plays no other role than the role of naming the already received sense impressions. The received sense impressions are independent of language with respect to their existence as well as to their nature and structure. Language presupposes the non-linguistic reality it is a language about in the same sense in which a name presupposes the existence of that which the name is naming.

According to Kant the relation between language and the non-linguistic reality language is about is different. Because to Kant language plays a decisive role, not for the bare existence of the non-linguistic reality but for its structure. The reasons for this essential role of language are that, according to Kant, concepts are necessary tools of comprehending the non-linguistic reality and that concepts can be displayed only through language. The basic and fundamental element of language is, all according to Kant, the judgment, i.e., a proposition in which a predicate is predicated of a subject. To pass judgments (i.e. to apply concepts) is the function of the understanding. It is the function of the understanding, through its concepts, to comprehend (to conceive) the non-linguistic reality. Which is the same as to say that it is language which enables us to comprehend and conceive the non-linguistic reality.

It is essential to understand that since the concepts are expressions of the function of the understanding and it is the

concepts which determine the structure of the non-linguistic
reality - how it appears as the facts experienced, - it follows
that the comprehended and experienced reality (to repeat: that
reality whose structure is determined by concepts) is different
from the reality not conceptually determined. It is the reality
which not only is unknown but also, since it is only through
concepts that reality can be known, unknowable. The known and
experienced object is thus different with respect to form and
structure from the unknown and unexperienced object. Reality as
it appears when conceived by concepts Kant calls the world of
appearance. The object as it is when not conceived through
concepts Kant calls the thing in itself.

Kant makes a distinction between what he calls empirical
concepts and categories. Empirical concepts are concepts which
enable me to comprehend the things I observe as being of a
certain kind. The concept of a fly enables me to conceive of this
particular insect as a fly. The concept of a moon is likewise an
empirical concept; without this concept I would not conceive this
particular celestial object as a moon. By categories, however,
Kant understands concepts which constitute the very
presuppositions for having and using empirical concepts. They
consequently constitute the presuppositions - the necessary
conditions - for all comprehension, experience, consciousness,
and consequently, language.

Let us examine one of the categories, the category of
substance. Hume, as we have seen, denied the existence of a
substance in the sense in which a substance is the bearer of the
properties of an object and therefore itself a propertyless entity.
Kant agrees with Hume that there is no such entity. Substance
is not an ontological entity but a category. It is a concept
constituting a necessary condition for comprehending anything as

anything. It is a necessary condition for experience and a necessary condition for language.

Instead of language presupposing sense impressions we now have that the experienced object - the object constituting experience, the object of consciousness - presupposes language. Or expressed differently: The logical structure of language determines the existence of facts.[4]

If one compares Hume's view of the function of language with Kant's view, it is, obviously, Hume's view which coincides with the common-sense view whereas Kant's view is opposed to it. To be in accordance with common-sense does not require a justification; to be opposed to it does. Hume, therefore, does not need a justification whereas Kant does.

As we have seen, it is the use of the categories which constitutes the necessary conditions for knowledge and experience; without the categories consciousness could have no empirical content. Such use constitutes a necessary but not a sufficient condition. The use of categories and, consequently, the use of language is possible only under the condition of what Kant calls the unity of consciousness, or as he also calls it the transcendental apperception, or the transcendental unity of consciousness. The term 'transcendental' is important. It emphasizes that the unity of consciousness or of apperception is a condition for having consciousness. If there were no such unity of consciousness from one moment to the next there would be no consciousness at all. This unity is not a psychological fact; it cannot be an object of psychological observation, because it would presuppose that the transcendental unity itself was part of the content of consciousness; but since it is a condition for having consciousness at all, it follows that it cannot also be one of the objects of consciousness - one of the objects it conditions. The transcendental apperception or the transcendental unity of consciousness is a fact which follows from the logic of the concept of consciousness.

That this is the case can, among other ways, be seen as follows. Suppose I say something by uttering the sentence 'p.' The very moment I begin the uttering of this sentence I already know what I am going to say. I do not acquire knowledge of what I am saying by listening to my own words as I have to listen to the words of another person in order to acquire knowledge of what he is saying. In fact, I am not listening to my own words at all. If I were, my listening would split my consciousness into two consciousnesses - one which was engaged in saying something and one which was engaged in listening to what was being said. To speak and to listen are two different activities which cannot be executed consciously by one and the same person at one and the same time. A condition for knowing what I am saying while saying it is consequently that I am one consciousness and not two, - a condition which is already packed into the word 'I.' Connected with this condition is the condition that I am able to hold together that which is intended to be said during the saying of it; or expressed differently, to preserve a unity of consciousness while saying it. It is, as just mentioned, this unity of consciousness which is expressed by the use of the word 'I.' The personal identity which is presupposed by any speech act and therefore also by any act of consciousness is thus presupposing the use of the word 'I'.

Another way to see the necessity of the transcendental apperception is this. Suppose that consciousness was a combination of, so to speak, atoms of consciousness. What this would mean is that, at each moment, the content of consciousness was unconnected with the content of the previous moment as well as that of the succeeding moment. And to say that it is unconnected is to say that at each moment there is no knowledge whatsoever of the content of consciousness of any other moment. If this were so, it would mean that there were just as many instances of consciousness as the number of atoms of consciousness constituting a certain consciousness. Which is the same as to say that there would be just as many different uses of the word 'I' as there are atoms of consciousness. The ordinary use of the word 'I' would thus lose its meaning. It is here presupposed that there is consciousness connected with each moment - with each atom of consciousness. But even this presupposition cannot hold. Each moment must be thought of as an extensionless point in time. If it were not so, that, in other words, each moment had a certain duration, we might still maintain that during that period there were a unity of consciousness. But could there be a non-time consuming instance of consciousness? At first the answer seems to be an affirmative one. In these post-Rylean and post-Wittgensteinian days we realize that many mental verbs are achievement verbs and that many expressions which seem to be used to describe or to refer to a mental act really have a quite different function. But in the situation now under consideration no mental verb can be applied at all. It is a situation in which an atom of consciousness exists only the very instance (a non-time consuming instant) it is created. A condition of speaking of consciousness is that one knows what one is conscious of. Whatever the content of consciousness is, one can only have knowledge of it through one's conceptual system, i.e. through a language. And since language has to be learned, and since learning is a time consuming process, it follows that there can be no consciousness in our alleged atoms of consciousness. Because at no time could a language have been learned and, consequently, at no time could consciousness have arisen.

Furthermore, to assume the existence of in time unextended atoms of consciousness affords well-known paradoxes. Thought seems compelled to assume the existence of the unextended point in time - the point referred to by the word 'now.' If the point in time referred to by the word 'now' were extended there would have to be a point during that extended time where half of it already had elapsed, which means that it already belonged to the past, and where the other half of it had not yet occurred and thus belongs to the future. The point in time referred to by the word 'now' thus has to be without extension.[5] But such a point in time can as little be part of time as, say, a mathematical point can be part of a line. It cannot be what we are inclined to think it must be, an atom of time, i.e. that which constitutes time. Time cannot be a sum of such atoms - it can be that as little as my fortune can be a sum of an indefinite class of zeros.

On the one hand we seem to be compelled to maintain that time consists of unextended 'nows.' On the other hand it is realized that if this were the case there could be no time at all. Applied to consciousness we get a similar paradox. To be conscious entails that one is conscious **now**. The thought I had a moment ago I do not have now. And the thought I have right now is not the thought I shall have the next moment. The thought of the next moment, i.e. the moment which is still future, obviously cannot now constitute an object of my consciousness. But if the present now (the specious present) is the only time in which I can justifiably be said to exist as a conscious being, the paradoxical conclusion must be that I do not exist as a conscious being. I cannot have consciousness of my own existence. The 'now' (the specious present) is not part of time. Either it has not yet arrived, or it has already passed. But since the fact is, however, that I am conscious right now, it follows that consciousness cannot be a sum of unextended atoms of consciousness. There must be a unity of consciousness stretching from one moment to the next moment. If there were no unity of consciousness such that consciousness remained one and the same consciousness - the same in the sense that the person using the first person pronoun singular uses it as an expression of personal identity, - if there were no such unity there could be neither consciousnes nor language. It is this insight which Kant expresses in his famous saying: "It must be possible for the 'I think' to accompany all my representations; for otherwise something would be represented in me which could not be thought at all, and that is equivalent to saying that the representation would be impossible, or at least would be nothing to me."[6]

Since the concept of the transcendental apperception and the concept of the I are inseparable, it follows that the I as a condition of consciousness cannot itself be part of the content of consciousness. Kant consequently calls it the transcendental Ego. Nor is the transcendental Ego one of the categories. It is that which constitutes the foundation for their existence and their use. None of the categories, therefore, can be applied to it. Which is the same as to say that it is logically impossible that it ever could be an object of knowledge.

Since the transcendental Ego - the I in the 'I think' - must remain the same I from one moment to the next moment, it seems implied that the I must be a kind of entity or a substance. But that this is not entailed by the concept of the transcendental apperception Kant thinks he can show by the following thought experiment.[7] Imagine, so he says, that we have a series of elastic balls. The first of these balls is endowed with consciousness and when it hits the second one it transmits not only its motion to this other ball but also its consciousness. When the second ball hits the third ball the same thing happens, and so on until the last ball of the series it hit. This last ball will thus have received the consciousness of all the preceding ones and will consequently regard them as its own consciousness. It is, so the last ball will infer, one and the same consciousness. In a sense, this inference is correct. Since the consciousness of the last ball possesses the memories of all the preceding balls and, referring back to these, will use the term 'I' to refer to these preceding ones, it is what we mean by 'one and the same consciousness.' But it is not correct if the expression 'one and the same consciousness' is meant to refer to an entity or substance which has remained one and the same during this period. It ought to be noticed, however, that Kant's argument, for all its ingenuity, does not quite show what he intends it to show. Since each ball possesses consciousness during the period stretching from the moment it is hit to the moment it transmits it to the next ball – and this period must have some duration, however short – it follows that during that period there is a consciousness which is one and the same consciousness and whose identity cannot itself be experienced in analogy with the rolling balls. But even though Kant's argument falls short of showing what it is supposed to show, it of course does not entail the truth of that which the argument is an argument against. That would still be fallacious according to Kant's fundamental view, namely, that the transcendental apperception – the transcendental Ego – is the ultimate condition for the use of the categories and therefore cannot be conceived by them. That would make that which conditions the conditioned to be conditioned by that which it itself conditions.

With Kant, Hume's fundamental model of the relation between language and reality has been radically changed and the catastrophic consequences of Hume's philosophy have been avoided. Instead of the mystical substance as a bearer of properties, and therefore itself propertyless, and which Hume, quite correctly, thought was a meaningless assumption, but, incorrectly, thought could be discarded, Kant introduced substance, not as an ontological entity, but as a category. And instead of the mystical I of which Hume was unable to get any sense-impression Kant introduced the transcendental apperception or the transcendental unity of consciousness expressed through the 'I think,' and which constitutes a condition of consciousness. As a condition of consciousness, and consequently not an object of consciousness, Kant's 'I' thus becomes the transcendental I or transcendental Ego. It is an Ego which can be conceived neither by the category of substance nor by any other of the categories, including the category of unity.

Although Kant succeeded in escaping the catastrophic consequences of Hume's philosophy, his own philosophy seems to entail a serious, not to say fatal, problem. It is a problem connected with the transcendental apperception as the condition for the employment of the categories and, accordingly, for all knowledge, experience, and consciousness. It is the problem of the thing in itself. The stuff - the matter on which the categories are employed, - is **in itself** logically cut off from being an object of all possible cognition.

To accept such a view - a view which seems to be logically forced upon us - is nevertheless to accept an epistemologically and a metaphysically unsatisfactory, not to say impossible, situation. It splits the world into two worlds: the world formed and conceived by the forms of intuition (i.e., by the a priori forms of space and time) and the categories, and the world as it is in itself. But to assume even the existence of the world in itself is impossible without illegitimately borrowing from the forms and the categories. And yet, it seems inescapable to assume just such an existence. To employ categories implies applying them to something; and to say that the categories are employed to something implies that the something to which they are applied already is there as a candidate for being an 'object' - a something - to which the categories can be applied. It seems to be embedded in the concept of a category that there is a world to which the category can be applied. In other words, it is possible in thought to separate the categories and that to which they are applied. Or rather, although it seems possible, it seems to be so only partly. Because one of the separated elements - that to which the categories are supposed to be applied - cannot be imagined or conceived at all. This in itself is not fatal. What is fatal is the reason why it cannot be imagined or conceived. It is surely not because our imagination is not powerful enough and, consequently, due to a weakness or defect on our part. The reason it cannot be imagined is simply that there is nothing to imagine. The 'it' which cannot be imagined is logically excluded from having a meaning since it is logically excluded that the conditions for having a meaning can be satisfied - the conditions, namely, that the categories already are applied. And this is precisely what, according to the logic of the situation, they are not.

Whereas the arguments for the transcendental apperception as well as the arguments for the existence of categories seem cogent, the assumption of the existence of the thing in itself is not. At the same time it is an assumption which it is difficult to escape. It is concerning this untenable logical situation that Jacobi states that he is confused since, as he says, **"without** that assumption I could not enter the system, and **with** it I could not remain in it."[8]

The three concepts crystalized in the Kantian system and which constitutes its conceptual model are thus: (1) The transcendental apperception, or the transcendental unity of consciousness, or the transcendental ego; (2) the categories; and (3) the thing in itself. Of these three concepts (1) seems to constitute a necessary condition and is thus unavoidable. Also (2) seems to be unavoidable in so far as it is an epistemological fact that knowledge, experience and language depend on categories, although it may indeed be debated whether Kant's arguments for the particular twelve categories, whose existence he claims to have discovered and whose necessity he thinks he has proved (by the so-called transcendental deduction), are correct. That (3) is unacceptable has just been explained. It is this third concept, the concept of the thing in itself, which made it impossible to accept the Kantian system as the final, or even a cogent system. Not only did it entail a meaningless concept, it also resulted in the paradoxical situation that the reality, the knowledge of which must be the ultimate purpose for any epistemology and metaphysics, is utterly unknowable.

Two, and only two, possibilities seem to be available. If it is the case that the transcendental apperception necessitates the concept of the thing in itself the Kantian system must be discarded. This is a difficult, if not impossible, thing to do since precisely the transcendental apperception as well as the existence and application of categories seem unavoidable. The remaining possibility, then, is to accept the transcendental apperception and the existence and application of categories but to attempt to avoid the apparent necessity of the thing in itself. Obviously, such an attempt is by no means easy. If the transcendental apperception and the existence and application of the categories are accepted the conclusion which one seems compelled to accept is that the so-called stuff to which the categories are applied, and which already must exist prior to their application, in its independent

existence, i.e.   before the categories are applied, must be
classified as unknowable.

Nevertheless, what absolute idealism is attempting to do is
precisely to eliminate the thing in itself from the Kantian
philosophy. No other possibility seems available. Absolute idealism
did not doubt that the transcendental apperception is a necessary
condition for knowledge, and did not doubt that knowledge and
experience is determined by categories. But since the concept of
the thing in itself is a contradictory concept, absolute idealism had
to find a way of eliminating it.

Both Hume and Kant were dualists. Hume is a dualist with
respect to his conception and role of language. There is a
language and there is that which language is about. Kant's
dualism is more complicated. Admittedly, there is an expressed
dualism between phenomena (i.e. the objects and facts structured
and determined by the categories) and the thing in itself or the
stuff on which the categories are applied. But difficulties appear
if this dualism is translated into a problem of the relation between
language and the non-linguistic reality language is about. On the
one hand, language must be about a non-linguistic reality; if it
were not, it would not be a language at all; but on the other
hand, it cannot be about a non-linguistic reality, because the
non-linguistic reality, understood as that which exists
independently of and prior to language, is, and must be, utterly
unknown. Nothing can be said about it at all. According to the
Kantian conceptual model, language can only be about that which
the categories of language already have conceptually structured
and determined. Or, in other words, language is about something
which, in the last analysis, is a reflexion of itself - or, to use a
Hegelian expression, is about itself in its otherness.

In other words, in order to eliminate the **enfant terrible** of the Kantian philosophy: The concept of the thing in itself, philosophy seems compelled to accept the existence of a certain dialectical situation. According to the very concept of a language it must be something different from itself; at the same time an understanding of the relation between language and its object shows that this is not the case. This dialectical tension, between to be different and yet not to be different (identity between that which cannot be identical), is a basic problem with Fichte, Schelling, and Hegel.

Through the necessity of purifying Kantianism from the concept of the thing in itself the background for the philosophy of absolute idealism is set. Through the attempt to solve the dialectical tension, the tension between on the one hand consciousness, the I, and language, and on the other hand the object of consciousness, the non-I, and the object of language (i.e. that which language is about), its theme is given.

Through this, admittedly, somewhat simplified characterization or sketch of its background and problems the stage is set for the philosophy of absolute idealism.

Fichte

The First but Decisive Step of Absolute Idealism

Kant's philosophy had, as could be expected, an enormous impact on the contemporary philosophical culture. But almost all philosophers, also those who were the greatest admirers of his philosophy, understood that it could survive only under the condition that the concept of the thing in itself was rendered harmless. In the philosophic debate toward the end of the 18th century participated such renowned philosophers as the earlier mentioned Friedrich Heinrich Jacobi, Gottlob Ernst Schulze (also known under the name Anesidemus, a pseudonym he used for his first book, published in 1792) who hardly, however, can be characterized as a Kantian, Karl Leonhard Reinhold, and Salomon Maimon, probably the sharpest thinker of them all.[9]

It was Johann Gottlieb Fichte, however, who succeeded in creating a system, which, according to his own opinion, was within the framework of Kantianism, but in fact was a new philosophic system, althought it originated from Kant's **Critique of Pure Reason**. Fichte regarded his system as a deepening of the interpretation and the understading of Kant's philosophy rather than an as alteration of it. And in his **Lectures on the History of Philosophy**, Hegel says: "Fichte's philosophy is the completion of the Kantian philosophy" and, somewhat categorically, adds: "Besides these systems and Schelling's system there are no systems."[10] Kant, who to begin with backed Fichte up, later distanced himself from him.[11]

Nevertheless, despite Kant's protest and open letter, Fichte's system may with some justification be said to fall within the framework of Kantianism; the essential difference is, as indicated many times, that the concept of the thing in itself is eliminated. Admittedly, it is difficult to judge this change as a mere interpretation of the Critique; rather, it is a revision. In contrast to Jacobi who, as quoted above, maintained that without the concept of the thing in itself he could not get into the system, Fichte claimed that he could.

Consciousness, according to Fichte, is constituted by ideas. The term 'idea' must, in this connection, be taken to mean whatever can constitute the content of consciousness: The sensations of smell, of hearing, of seeing, and of touching are all ideas. There are two kinds of ideas. Partly there are the ideas we create ourselves (e.g. the thoughts I have when I am thinking of something, or when I am daydreaming), and partly the ideas whose existence are independent of my will (e.g. the content of my consciousness when I see, hear, smell, taste and touch something). This latter kind of ideas constitutes what we call experience. The ideas of experience are subjected to a necessity whose condition is independent of the will and freedom of the individual. What this condition is, it is the task of philsophy to find. Obviously, the condition of experience cannot itself be an object of experience.

To the question what this condition is, two entirely different answers are possible. These two answers constitute what Fichte terms respectively 'dogmatism' and 'idealism ' .

According to dogmatism the condition of experience is the thing in itself. The ultimate condition of experience is therefore something which is totally distinct from and in its existence totally independent of knowledge and experience. According to the ordinary interpretation of the Kantian concept of the thing in itself Kantianism must be interpreted as dogmatism. According to idealism, however, experience is conditioned, not by an alleged thing in itself, but is conditioned by, and has its ultimate source in, the intellect.

To the question which of these two possibilities one ought to choose, Fichte appears to maintain that it is up to the individual to choose as he prefers. There can be no compelling arguments for choosing one instead of the other. Neither idealism nor dogmatism can be falsified by experience. It is about this choice that one finds Fichte's often quoted statement that the choice depends on what kind of person one is.[12] However, if one looks more closely at what he is saying, it appears, as we shortly shall see, to be much less of a free choice. One must choose either dogmatism or idealism but not both. And to choose one alternative is to reject the other one. Dogmatism and idealism are two metaphysical theories; therefore it would be a misunderstanding of these theories to try to verify or falsify them through experience. There are other ways, however, of testing a metaphysical theory than through experience. Any conceptual system (and this is what a metaphysical system involves) has, due to the nature or logic of the concepts making up the system, certain conceptual consequences. As we have seen, the consequences of Hume's system were that concepts fundamental to any language had to be committed to the flames. The Kantian system had, among others, the consequence that it appeared to entail the concept of the thing in itself. And according to Fichte both dogmatism and idealism have consequences which make the choosing of one of them, at least to a considerable degree, a rational choice. The decisive concept is the concept of freedom. To choose dogmatism is, so Fichte maintains, to reject freedom, to choose idealism is to accept freedom.

Dogmatism explains the existence of experience and, consequently, the existence of consciousnes, which in turn explains the existence of the I, by help of the thing in itself. It is the thing in itself which constitutes the ultimate ground of experience and therefore also of consciousness and the I. According to Fichte, however, there is one proposition which cannot be doubted, the proposition, namely, that the I is independent and free. But if dogmatism is true, the consequence would be that the I, regarding both its acts and its existence, would be dependent on that which in itself is without consciousness and consequently also be without freedom. The result would therefore be that there would be no freedom. Fichte's claim presupposes the, in itself rather plausible, principle that the existence of consciousness and a free I cannot be the effect of something without consciousness and freedom. And since he takes the freedom of the I for granted, it follows that dogmatism is false. It is not just a contingent fact but a necessity that we employ such verbs as 'to choose', 'to decide', 'to accept' and 'to reject'. That the existence and use of such verbs are a necessity is of course not denied by the dogmatist. What he will assert, however, is that the employment of these verbs can be explained from a deterministic point of view. Not only can the fact that I happen to be in a situation which requires that I make a decision (i.e. employ the verb 'to decide') be explained deterministically; and not only is this very explanation itself explained deterministically, and so on infinitely, but also the acceptance of this is deterministic. However, by conceiving all these verbs as deterministic by nature the dogmatist transcends the logic of language. What we mean by the claim that the I is free is, and is nothing but, the claim that there are situations in which such (and kindred) verbs can be correctly employed. And if we deny it, i.e. if we accept the view of the dogmatist, we cannot avoid an infinite regress. Because it requires that our acceptance of the deterministic explanation itself is explained deterministically which explanation in turn has to be accepted. And this last mentioned acceptance also has to be explained deterministically, which explanation has to be accepted, etc. etc.

As mentioned above, Fichte maintains that whether one chooses dogmatism or idealism depends on what sort of person one is. By this famous dictum Fichte does not imply that ultimately the choice is not a rational choice. He does not maintain, therefore, that one choice is no more to be criticized than the other. That he does not imply this is implicit in his affirmation of freedom and the incompatibility between freedom and dogmatism; explicitly it is expressed in his condemnation of a dogmatist. About the dogmatist he says: "A person indolent by nature or dulled and distorted by mental servitude, learned luxury, and vanity will never raise himself to the level of idealism."[13] In other words, Fichte is not only condemning a person accepting dogmatism; he is also, at least by implication, maintaining that to choose dogmatism is an expression of insufficient thinking, - an insufficiency which apparently does not characterize the person who chooses idealism.

The fact that consciousness has a content which is created by consciousness itself (e.g. content created by imagination or that which we choose to think of) does not, at least not in the first instance, require any explanation; but it does require an explanation that consciousness has a content which is not created by itself. It requires an explanation that there is an object for consciousness (the subject or the Ego) which appears to be induced in consciousness independently of the subject. If dogmatism is false only idealism remains as the explanation and the ultimate condition of the existence of the object of experience or the non-Ego of experience.

At first glance such an explanation seems absurd and to constitute no explanation at all. If the Ego constitutes the explanation of both the content of consciousness - the ideas - which is created by consciousness itself (i.e. the ideas of our imagination and our thoughts) as well as the content which we could never say is created by consciousness itself (i.e. the content when we taste, see, hear, smell, and touch something), we are still in need of an explanation of the difference between the two kinds of content of consciousness - the two kinds of ideas.

The point, however, is this. When Fichte says that according to idealism the existence and structure of the ideas of experience are due to what he names the Ego, or the intelligence, or even the Absolute, he is not referring to the individual ego but to what he calls the universal Ego.

The concept of 'the universal Ego' may appear to be a contradictory concept. An ego, an I, is precisely what, by its very meaning, cannot be a universal. Whenever I use the word 'I', I use it to refer to or to identify a particular individual who at this particular time exists at this particular place. But this is only half the story. The other half - the one which is relevant in this context - is a descendant of Kant's transcendental apperception, which is to say that it refers to the necessary conditions for having any consciousness at all. These conditions are, needless to say, the same for each individual, - if they were not, they could not be the **necessary** conditions. To express it a bit grotesquely, my transcendental apperception is the same as everybody else's transcendental apperception. The transcendental apperception, or the transcendental unity of consciousness, Kant calls, as already mentioned, the transcendental Ego.[14]

The consciousness of each conscious being is an actualization which is conditioned by the transcendental Ego. The transcendental Ego thus is a universal Ego.

The transcendental Ego is the Ego Fichte maintained is the ultimate ground of all ideas of experience, i.e. of the content of consciousness which is not created by consciousness itself. It is the Ego which constitutes the condition for the categories of understanding and for the a priori principles of knowledge. It is consequently the Ego which Fichte maintains constitutes the ultimate foundation not only for consciousness and knowledge, but also for that which consciousness and knowledge is a consciousness and knowledge of; i.e., it is the ultimate foundation not only for the consciousness and knowledge but also for the object of consiousness and knowledge. However, by being the ultimate condition of consciousness and of the object of consciousness the transcendental or universal Ego must by necessity itself be without consciousness and cannot itself be an object of consciousness and knowledge. This was, of course, a heritage from Kant's doctrine that the transcendental unity of consciousness, being a condition for the application of the categories, cannot itself be an object to which the categories can be applied and therefore cannot be an object of knowledge.

Fichte's first task is to show how it is possible from the transcendental or universal Ego to deduce the different individual consciousnesses and the objects for these consciousnesses. His task is to show how it is possible to deduce what he calls the different limited and finite egos and the different objects, i.e. non-egos, for these different limited and finite egos.

Fichte maintains three principles are sufficient for such a deduction. The first principle is simply this: A is A. That A is identical with A seems a trivial, empty, and uninteresting truth, but also a truth which cannot be validated through other principles since its validity is presupposed in all other forms of proofs.

How is it possible for Fichte from such an empty principle to deduce (to prove) his rather pretentious metaphysical system? However, Fichte does not deduce his system from the **sentence** 'A is A,' or at least not from it alone. It is from the sentence in connection with the fact that the sentence is a statement which is made, - and statements do not make themselves; they are made only by individuals endowed with consciousness. The sentence itself is non-existential; from it nothing concerning the existence of A can be inferred. All the sentence is saying is that if there is such a thing as an A, then this A is identical with A. But since the sentence is used to make a statement, or a proposition, it follows that it is made by an individual who accepts it as valid (accepts, as Fichte says, that the relation or the law according to which we judge that the sentence 'A is A' is valid). The individual - the Ego - who accepts the validity of 'A is A' must therefore exist. The proposition 'I am' has consequently the same validity as the proposition 'A is A'. The difference is, however, that whereas the latter proposition is a hypothetical proposition, namely the proposition "If there is such a thing as an A it is identical with A," the proposition 'I am' is an existential proposition. It would have no meaning to say that if I exist then I am identical with myself; because my existence is a presupposition, not for the sentence 'A is A' but for my making it **and** for my accepting it.

Fichte's next move is the following. We now have two valid propositions, (i) the hypothetical proposition that 'A is A,' and (ii) the existential proposition 'I am'. We thus know that there is something which we can substitute for 'A', namely 'I'. By substituting 'I' for 'A' we get the existential (and consequently non-hypothetical) proposition 'I am I' or 'Ego is Ego'. This proposition is an expression of the formal structure of consciousness: The I knows and asserts its own identity, i.e. the identity (or in Kant's terminology, the transcendental unity of consciousness), which is a condition for having consciousness at all. Knowledge and the assertion of the proposition 'I am I' implies, furthermore, the formal structure of self-consciousness. Because the concept of self-consciousness implies, partly that there is a knowing I (subject), and partly that the I (the subject) is conscious of itself, knows and asserts itself as a knowing I or subject; or expressed differently, that the I or subject has itself as object.

Since, furthermore, the proposition 'I am I' is the existential form of the proposition 'A is A', it follows that the I as a knowing being is an absolute and free I. The proposition 'A is A' is, as already mentioned, a presupposition for all consciousness, thinking, and knowledge; it cannot, therefore, have its ground in anything else but the I. It is the I which posits its own existence and thereby actualizes a necessary condition for consciousness.[15] By expressing himself in this way Fichte ends up in almost insoluble problems, - problems connected with his use of the verb 'to posit'.

To say that the I posits itself seems to imply that the I performs an act; and to perform an act presupposes consciousness. But the I cannot possess consciousness before the conditions for possessing it are satisfied. If Fichte is interpreted as if the I in the distant past created its own consciousness by satisfying the conditions for consciousness, an impossible logical situation results. The Fichtean concept of positing must not be interpreted, therefore, in analogy with the concept of action. To act presupposes a consciousness, it presupposes a subject and an object. But, as Fichte himself points out, before the I posits itself neither subject nor object can have any existence. However, Fichte's philosophic system is not a system which purports to explain how consciousness has in fact developed. Fichte is trying neither to be a psychologist nor to be an anthropologist, he is not describing the actual history of the becoming of consciousness; as a philosopher he is instead laying down the logical conditions for the existence of the concept of consciousness. And the very first condition for this concept is that there is an I - an I which has identity with itself; it is an I, therefore, capable of asserting the proposition "I am I". Instead of speaking of an act performed by an I which before the act only misleadingly can be called an I - an act, therefore, through which something new is created, - one should speak of laying down the logical conditions for that which already has existence.

Although the proposition "I am I" is an expression of the logical structure of self-consciousness, some additional proposition(s) is obviously required. Because what the proposition expresses is only that the I is conscious of itself as a knowing subject. And if the I had knowledge of nothing else, if, in other words, the I (the subject) as its object had that it itself was a knowing subject, then something else would be required as an object of its knowledge. Because if the I as its object had nothing else than the fact that it was a knowing subject, an infinite regress was inescapable: I know that I know that I know that I know that I know that I know ad infinitum. To the question what it is that the I knows there could be only one answer, the answer namely, that I know. As an object of knowledge the I must therefore have something other than itself; it must have a non-I or a non-Ego. Fichte's explanation of the existence and the structure of the non-Ego constitutes the crucial point in his metaphysical system. It marks the decisive step which separates him from Kantianism; it lays out the path along which abolute idealism was going to proceed.

As we have seen, Hume's philosophic system leads to the negation of knowledge; Kant's system implies the contradictory (or meaningless) concept of the thing in itself. It was an inevitable result since, according to Kantianism, the a priori forms of knowledge entailed that the so-called stuff of knowledge existed independently of the forms (if it did not the forms had nothing to form). In order to find a logical model - a conceptual scheme - which entailed neither absurdities nor contradictions it is necessary to change the premises of respectively Hume's and Kant's philosophy. But how is this possible? Are there indeed other possibilities? Is it not the case that metaphysical thinking with respect to its main problem has reached a limit it seems impossible to transcend but which all the same has to be transcended unless metaphysics by conceptual necessity forever shall remain in the Platonic cave?

Fichte's ingenious, original and courageous, even daring attempt at a solution is to assert that even though the object of my consciousness, (the paper on which I write, the stars I see on the firmament, and the spider I step on), is something which is different from me - to deny it would be an expression of insanity, - it nevertheless is the case that there is a sense according to which it is correct to say that the object, or better, the objective world, is created by the I. As just mentioned, to assert this is an expression not only of the creativity of a genius but also of metaphysical courage or daring. Nevertheless, it may, after all, perhaps not be so daring as it seems to be. Because the I in which, according to Fichte, the objective world has its (logical or conceptual) root is obviously not anybody's individual I. The 'I' referring to an individual, i.e. to the person who uses the word 'I', to the person existing in space and time, is the so-

called empirical I or empirical ego. It is the Ego which is
determined by contingent circumstances; that is, circumstances
which exist as a matter of fact but which do not exist by logical
necessity. That I am born on a specific day of a particular year,
that I have had the experiences and, consequently, memories as I
in fact have had, and, in general, have had the life I happen to
have had, are contingent facts. Any person's empirical I must by
necessity be different from the empirical I of anybody else. No
two persons can have exactly the same memories, experiences,
and, in general, the same content of consciousness. But besides
the empirical self there is the universal self. Common to all
conscious beings is that they satisfy the necessary conditions for
having consciousness. These conditions, which, as already
mentioned, are descendants of Kant's transcendental apperception,
are universal, i.e. they are universally valid and shared by all
human beings. While all human beings have their own individual
empirical ego they all share the same universal Ego.

Fichte's 'I am I' has often been compared to Descartes' famous
'I think, therefore I am' (**Cogito ergo sum**). There is, however,
a decisive difference between Descartes' and Fichte's use of these
sentences. Descartes' I, the existence of which he cannot doubt,
is his own individual empirical I.   From this empirical I (his
thoughts and doubts) he infers the existence of his own non-
empirical soul-substance (his **res cogitans**).   When Descartes
pronounces his "**Cogito ergo sum**" it is not, admittedly, an
empirical and contingent proposition; in fact, it is not a
proposition which can be used on par with other sentences or
propositions.   Propositions such as: "There are lions in Africa"
and "The Greenland whale does no longer exist" are propositions
whose truth can be empirically tested.   But it has no meaning to
attempt to test the proposition "I exist".   The very utterance of
the proposition obviously presupposes the existence of the person

who utters it. But even if the proposition is not a contingent proposition, the fact that the person who utters it exists is a contingent fact. In other words: The proposition "I exist" as it was used by Descartes is a contingent proposition. Or rather, it is not a proposition within a language but a proposition expressing a presupposition for the use of any language at all. The proposition "It is a fact that the person Descartes refers to by the term 'I' exists" is a contingent proposition. From Descartes' proposition "I think, therefore I am" the existence of other minds does not follow.

Fichte's proposition "I am I" is entirely different. It is not a proposition asserting Fichte's own existence. It is not a proposition about the empirical I; it is a proposition about the universal I. Fichte's proposition has thus another meaning and possesses other logical properties than the Cartesian proposition. The existence of the I Fichte speaks about is not a contingent fact. The universal I constitutes the necessary conditions for consciousness as such; and as we later shall see, they are the necessary conditions not only for all consciousness but also for whatever is, i.e. for what in metaphysical language is termed Being. And even though it may be maintained that it is a contingent fact that there are beings endowed with consciousness, it is not a contingent fact that there is anything at all, or, if one wants, that Being is. If one accepts the Kantian categories Reality and Existence (**Realität und Dasein**), accepts in other words that they are necessary conditions for knowledge, thinking, consciousness, and, therefore, for language, it follows, that it is conceptually impossible to think that there is nothing. The sentence "Being does not exist" is not a contradiction, it is meaningless. The classical question: "Why is there something and not just nothing?" presupposes that the thought of absolute nothingness, i.e. the non-existence of any kind of world, has meaning - which, at least from a Kantian point of view, it does not have.

How does Fichte argue for his view that the object of consciousness, in the last analysis, is posited by the I? We saw how Fichte through his first principle, the principle that A is identical with A, thought that he could validate his proposition that the I posits itself. His second principle is that non-A is not equal to A. The sentence 'Non-A is not equal to A' is of course different from the sentence 'Non-A is equal to non-A'. The latter sentence has the same logical form as the sentence 'A is equal to A' and thus expresses the very opposite of the former sentence. The sentence 'Non-A is not equal to A' expresses the logical truth that the negation of A is different from A whereas the sentence 'Non-A is equal to non-A' expresses the logical truth that the negation of A is equal to the negation of A.

The sentence 'Non-A is not equal to A' is, just as is the sentence 'A is equal to A', of a hypothetical nature. What it says is therefore this: 'If there is a non-A then it is not equal to A'. What does exist is the I which is able to accept the validity of the sentence. Which is the same as to say that the I in question, i.e. the I which posits itself and which is able to posit its own opposite, presupposes the identity of consciousness and, consequently, also self-consciousness. It is not just the case, however, that the I is able to posit itself; it is also able to posit its own opposite; the positing of its own opposite is entailed by the positing of itself. Because not only is the I a presupposition for the positing of the non-I, but the non-I is at the same time a presupposition for the I. Self-consciousness involves that I am conscious of myself as a conscious being. But in order to avoid the earlier mentioned infinite regress it is necessary to presuppose that the I as an object of consciousness has something else than itself as a conscious being.

What we so far have seen is this. Consciousness presupposes an I. An I is an I only if it is an I which is identical with itself, (i.e. the unity of consciousness or, expressed in Kantian terms, the transcendental apperception). It is consequently an I which entails self-consciousness. This, according to Fichte, is the unconditioned beginning and ultimate foundation of metaphysics. The unconditioned cannot be the facts of the external world; it must by necessity be rooted in consciousness - the consciousness without which the facts of the external world would not be facts. But to say that the first and unconditioned principle of consciousness is its identity with itself is the same as to say that this unconditioned foundation of consciousness is an identity which is posited by the I itself, (if it could be posited by something else it was not the unconditioned condition).

Fichte now introduces a third principle. The reason for doing this is an apparent conflict between the first and second principle. The universal or infinite I posits a non-I. But since the non-I is the negation of the I, the non-I appears to be a threat against the universality and infinity of the I. Nevertheless, it is a necessary condition for the existence of the I that the non-I also has existence. Expressed differently: Consciousness requires a principle (the non-I) which seems to negate consciousness - consciousness requires a principle which nullifies the presupposition for its existence. And if consciousness, i.e. the I, does not exist, then, according to Fichte's second principle, nor does the non-I. In order to solve this conflict Fichte introduces the concept of limitation (**Einschränkung**). To limit something is to negate it and thus to abolish some (but only some) of its reality. The posited I and the posited non-I limit each other through a partial abolishment of their reality. The concept of limitation consequently implies the concept of divisibility. The third principle, i.e. the principle

which, according to Fichte, solves the conflict between the first
and the second principle - thus is this. The I posits itself as a
divisible I and it posits the non-I as a divisible non-I. We thus
have: (i) The universal I (universal, infinite, and indivisible);
(ii) the divisible I, posited by the universal and indivisible I;
and finally (iii) the divisible non-I, likewise posited by the
universal and indivisible I. The divisible I constitutes individual
consciousnesses, and the divisible non-I constitutes the
(divisible) world, i.e. the different objects for the different
consciousnesses.

Fichte formulates his principles in a metaphysical language
and in a terminology hardly acceptable to modern philosophic
thought. It would therefore be useful, if possible, to translate
Fichte's classical metaphysical language into the language of
today's philosophy. Whether or not one agrees with Strawson's
claim, in his book **Individuals**, that no philosopher understands
his predecessors before he has rethought their thoughts in his
own terms.[16] To do so in the case of Fichte's philosophy would
indeed be a great help for a better understanding of the
metaphysical problem occupying him and of his principles, and for
creating a better appreciation of his ingenuity.

Philosophy has been increasingly aware of the relationship
between language and consciousness. Consciousness, in the sense
in which consciousness implies self-consciousness, is conditioned
by language. An examination of the logical structure of
consciousness, its categories and conditions, is accordingly
identical with an examination of the logical structure of language,
its categories and conditions.

Let me begin by an examination, or rather a translation, of
Fichte's first principle: The I posits itself. A language is by
necessity something which is spoken (or, in case of dead

languages, has been spoken). A language presupposes a speaker, and a speaker is a person who identifies himself (the only person who can do so) by the use of the word 'I'. The concept of 'I' has existence only if there is a language. Obviously, before there was any language no being could identify itself by help of the word 'I'. Or to express it in a way which may sound provoking, before there was any language no being was an I. Only language-using beings have an I. Neither dogs nor spiders can be an I, (even though they can be a you, a he, or a she). The existence of the I (the 'positing' of the I) is entailed by, and entailed by nothing but a language. But if language posits the I (the divisible, i.e. the individual I) and if the I posits the I, it follows that language should be identified as the I - the I, not as an individual I, but as the universal I. As already mentioned, Fichte's universal I or Ego is a descendant of Kant's transcendental apperception, which is the same as to say that the universal I, just as the transcendental apperception, is the unconditioned condition for all consciousness, or rather, the unconditioned condition for any language and, accordingly, the unconditioned condition for the existence of the divisible and individual I.

Should it be objected that it is a conceptual error to use the term 'I' in connection with the unconditioned condition for an I, the objection might seem to be valid, but it is only seemingly so. Because, as argued in the preceeding pages, there are uses of the word I whose meaning cannot be identified with anything in space and time identifiable. The meaning of such a use of the word 'I' can be neither identified with, nor defined in terms of, the body of the speaker or the psychological data. The word 'I' is consequently used in two different ways: Partly to identify the person who exists in space and time and who is different from all other persons, and partly to refer to the universal I, i.e., an I

which constitutes the condition, the condition not only for the
possibility that the individual speaker - the individual I - can
have a language, but also for the possibility of having any
language at all.

Let me next examine Fichte's second principle, i.e. the
principle that the I posits the non-I. Analogously to the
conceptual fact that to be conscious is to be conscious of
something, or in other words that consciousness in order to be
consciousness requires an object. Language, in order to be a
language, must describe, refer to, or be about something.
Language must have an object. An alleged language whose
function it is not to talk about or to be about something different
from itself is not a language. It is a logical problem, a problem
which shall not be dealt with here, whether and under which
circumstances a language can be a language about itself. It is
not a problem, however, that a language can be about another
language. The language which another language is about is
called an object-language, and the language which is about the
object-language is called a meta-language. These two languages,
the meta-language and the object-language, may be the same
natural language. It is of course quite possible to talk about the
English language in English. Although it is, from one point of
view, an employment of only one language, namely English, it is,
from a logical point of view, an employment of two languages: A
meta-language and an object-language.

But even though a language can be used to talk about
another language, which other language itself can be a language
about a third language, and so on, it is necessary that sooner or
later there is an object language which is not itself a meta-
language but is a language about a non-linguistic reality. The
series of languages which are about languages can be an infinite
series as little as can the series of, e.g., mirror images. A

mirror image can be a mirror image of another mirror image which in turn can be a mirror image of yet another mirror image and so on indefinitely but not infinitely. Sooner or later there must be a mirror image which is not a mirror image of a mirror image but is a mirror image of something which is only mirrored.[17]

But what, then, is this non-linguistic reality which language is about? If language is used to say something about a cat lying on a mat then the cat is the non-linguistic reality which the sentence "The cat is on the mat" is about. But how to describe or characterize this non-linguistic object which the sentence is about? Simply by saying that it is a cat. In other words I am caught or imprisoned in language. The non-linguistic reality required in order that a language can be a language can be neither thought, conceived, or, obviously, described, or characterized without a language. It may, perhaps, be objected that even though it is impossible to describe or to characterize the non-linguistic reality outside a language, then, it is possible to **identify** it. It is possible to point to it saying "this." But this objection is not valid. In order to identify that which is pointed to one must be able to see, hear, or in some other way, through the sense organs, conceive it. However, one can neither see or hear without seeing or hearing something. And to identify this something is to identify it **as** something. I am able to identify the animal I see lying on the mat because I am able to see that it is a cat, - I identify it as a cat. A necessary condition for being able to identify an animal as a cat is the possession of the concept 'cat'. If one does not know what a cat is one is unable to identify an animal as a cat. And to know what something or other is implies that one is able to apply the proper words and expressions concerning that which one has knowledge of.[18]

But if the non-linguistic reality can be conceived, thought, described, known and identified only by being encapsulated in a

language and thereby having its character as something non-
linguistic cancelled, what, then, becomes of the non-linguistic
reality which is a necessary condition for a language to be a
language?   If it is maintained that something non-linguistic
remains, then one is precluded from conceiving, describing,
knowing, understanding, identifying, or even to give any
meaning to it.   In other words, it would be a return to the
conceptual model which it was the purpose to escape: the
contradictory or even meaningless concept of the thing in itself.
It would be a 'something' which under no circumstances could be
an object of language; it could not be that which language is
about.

However, if it is the case that the non-linguistic reality
which language is about is captured or imprisoned by language -
has taken on the essence of language - it seems inevitable, in
analogy with Fichte's I which posits the non-I, to assert that
language 'posits' its own object; language posits the non-linguistic
reality.

Since a language is a language only if it is, or has been,
spoken, and since, furthermore, a language-user, and only a
language-user, ultimately can identify himself only by the use of
the word 'I', it follows that it is the I which posits language and,
consequently, also posits the non-linguistic reality. Which is the
same as to say that the I posits the non-I. It must be clarified,
however, what is meant by saying that the I posits language and,
accordingly, also posits the non-linguistic reality.

A language user is, so to speak, born into a certain, i.e.
an empirically given, language. He does not construct his own
language; instead he learns the language already in existence. It
is possible, therefore, to distinguish, on the one hand, the
language already in existence, i.e. the language each language

user learns, it is the language as such; and, on the other hand, the language of each individual language user, the language spoken by each individual language user. This latter is not the language already in existence, but the language he has learned to master. This is a distinction, therefore, between the language as such and the indefinite number of more or less imperfect instances of the language as such, i.e. the language over which the individual language user has more or less incomplete command. By the language as such (e.g. English as such) is understood the total number of words and the complete syntax of the language. It would be the language as it would be spoken by a (presumably non-existing) person who had a complete and perfect command over the language in question. The language as such enjoys logical priority over the language spoken by each individual language user; because without the language as such there would be no language to learn.

It is of course possible to construct a new language. It presupposes, however, an already existing language by help of which the new language is constructed. To construct a language from scratch, i.e. to construct it without the help of an already existing language, is a conceptual impossibility. Because the construction itself is a process which requires consciousness. And as maintained several times, without a language there can be no consciousness. The thinking required in order to do the construction is possible only with language as a means.

But if an already existing language is a presupposition for each individual language using being - the language he learns - it is necessary in order to avoid an infinite regress to assume that the language has developed during pre-historic times. The claim that language has come into existence during a pre-historic development is the same as to claim that man has been actualized as conscious being through a pre-historic development. How

language in fact has developed can of course only be subject to
more or less educated guesses.[19] Obviously, no written or other
possible evidence of consciousness can be used as tests. If **per
impossibili** such evidence could be found it would only prove that
language as means of communication already had become a reality
and, consequently, cannot be a testimony of the condition **before**
language came into existence. However, it remains a fact that
sometime at the dawn of times consciousness and language did
develop. It is at this point in time that the logical conditions for
consciousness and language were satisfied, that the I posits itself
as an I and at the same time posits the non-I. Or expressed
differently, the logical conditions for consciousness and language
(variously designated as the transcendental apperception, the
transcendental unity of consciousness, the transcendental Ego,
the Absolute Ego, the infinite and indivisible Ego) have always
existed although not always been actualized or satisfied. That the
conditions are satisfied is to say that language has been
actualized; it is to say, therefore, that the I (the ultimate
condition of language) posits itself (actualizes itself as an I or as
a language using being).

But if the non-linguistic reality is a concept which in itself
is of a linguistic nature (if the non-I is posited by the I) absurd
consequences seem to follow. It seems to imply that reality in
itself is of a linguistic nature. The dualism which is a
presupposition for the existence of a language - language must be
about a non-linguistic reality - ends up by negating itself. Or in
Fichte's language: The dualism which is a presupposition for
consciousness and therefore also for the existence of the I ends
up by negating itself. In both places, i.e. both between the I
and the non-I and between language and the non-linguistic
reality, there is a dialectical tension. The I entails a non-I. If
there were no non-I there would be no I either. In Fichte's

system the I and the non-I are at one and the same time both in opposition to each other and identical. They are in opposition to each other in as much as the I and the non-I would cancel each other if they did not limit each other. They are identical in as much as the non-I, which is posited by the I, must have a logical structure identical with the logical structure of the I. Or analogously: Language requires the non-linguistic reality. The paper on which I write and the pen with which I write are not, needless to say, linguistic entities. And, yet, only through language can I understand what the paper or the pen is.

Let me examine whether it is possible to overcome this dialectical tension and the seemingly absurd consequence that reality is a product of language. It would be absurd in the extreme to assert that before the existence of language using beings nothing whatever could have existence. It would be absurd in the extreme to assert that the existence of planets, mountains, and animals were brought about through language. It is important, however, to notice the following conceptual fact: Whatever exists must by necessity exist as something. It may be a stone, a tree, a spider, a certain chemical substance, a hydrogen atom, etc. etc. There are a great number of things, of course, of whose **whatness** there, so far, is no knowledge. But it nevertheless is the case that it is something. To assert that there is in existence something which does not exist as something is to make an assertion it is difficult not to call a contradiction. The consclusion is, therefore, that whatever is, whatever has existence, has a **whatness**; in other words, whatever exists is conceptually determined. And since concepts can be used only if there is a language, it follows that existence depends on language. It depends not only in the sense in which its **whatness** depends on it; it also depends on it in the sense of its bare existence. Language determines not just that something exists **as** something but also the bare fact **that** it exists. Suppose it is maintained that something exists of which nothing can be said. The reason nothing can be said is not due to ignorance; the reason is that there is nothing to be said. It would be what in older days' metaphysics was called pure being. And if pure being was supposed to have any being, i.e. to have ontological significance, it would be a conceptual fallacy. That it was a fallacy was clearly seen by Hegel and expressed in his famous dictum that pure being is nothing. In latter days' philosophy the same point has convincingly been argued by Russell in his famous and more technically worked out theory of description. According to this theory the use of the term 'existence' presupposes that whatever is said to exist, whatever is the subject of the grammatical predicate 'existence ', is conceptually determined. Being receives its being through language.

These arguments, however, emphasizes the above mentioned absurdity; they do not eliminate it as an absurdity: Nothing can exist before language is there to bestow existence upon it. Or differently expressed, language enjoys not only epistemological priority over that which language is about, it also enjoys ontological priority. It is important, however, to distinguish, not only between language as such and the individual instances of it, i.e. the language of the different individuals, but also to distinguish between what a certain period's language in fact covers, and what it, according to its logical powers, is capable of covering. Such a distinction does not imply the possibility of several radically different conceptual systems. If one assumes that the logical structure of our conceptual system is determined by categories, it follows that different conceptual systems, so far as their logical and categorial system is concerned, are identical. The language of the medieval ages as well as the language of today satisfy the conditions for being a language; they are conditioned by the same categories. But concepts which are conditioned by the development of the different sciences, the social structure, and the cultural development, are different. The language and thinking of the middle ages did not have at their disposal concepts such as proton, subconscious mind, and electricity. It would be absurd, however, to maintain that neither protons, the subconscious mind, nor electricity had any existence in the middle ages and that they did not come into being until the relevant scientific theories were advanced. Electricity existed before any physics existed. Electricity existed before it was discovered. It was discovered; it was not invented. The concepts through which the sciences of to-day and tomorrow are able to determine, for instance, electricity could have been applied if the sciences of yesterday had developed their conceptual system sufficiently. Electricity is nothing over and above the concepts through which the completed science (an idea which probably never will - or can - be realized)[20] determines it.

If the above arguments are accepted the inevitable conclusion - a conclusion which in a certain sense defines absolute idealism - must be that whatever is (e.g. electricity) is conditioned in its existence, not by any actualized language, but by the categories of language, i.e. by the logical conditions of language. Or expressed differently: **Nature and language (consciousness) are determined by the same logical categories and conditions. The logically impossible thought is also the logically impossible existence.** The being of being is determined by the same logical categories and conditions as is language and therefore also consciousness.

Fichte's statement that the infinite I posits the limited I and the limited non-I corresponds to the view that the logical categories determine (posit) the language of individuals as wells as that which these languages are about. Language as well as its object are both determined by the same logical conditions.

An important but unfortunately not sufficiently clarified concept of Fichte's philosophy is, as mentioned several times, the concept of positing. Fichte does not say that the limited I and the limited non-I are conditioned by the infinite I but that they are **posited** by it. The way Fichte uses the concept of positing is, it seems, in many respects similar or related to the concept of action. In fact, Fichte somewhere says that the infinite and unconditioned I performs the act of positing the I and the non-I.[21] But to conceive of the concept of positing as related to the concept of acting creates conceptual difficulties. An action presupposes, as already mentioned, a conscious being. Only beings with consciousness can act. Nature as such does not act; only persons act. The infinite and unlimited I, however, is neither a person nor a consciousness. The infinite and unlimited I (Kant's transcendental apperception) constitutes the logical condition for consciousness and, consequently, cannot itself have consciousness. The infinite and unlimited I cannot, therefore, perform any act. Moreover, to be conscious is by necessity to be conscious of something. Consciousness requires an object; but for the unlimited and infinite I there is no object - the object (the limited and finite non-I) is the result of the alleged act and, obviously, cannot constitute, therefore, the object before the act is finished. Accordingly, it is not possible, despite Fichte's words to the contrary, to interpret the verb 'to posit' in a way which involves the concept of an action. Fichte is well aware of the difficulties; but instead of dropping the concept of act he attempts an interpretation of the concept of consciousness according to which it would be meaningful to say of the infinite and unlimited I that it has consciousness.

Somewhere he says that the objection against the statement that the infinite I through an act posits the non-I can be met by assuming that there is a consciousness he characterizes as an immediate consciousness. It seems next to impossible, however, to attach any meaning to such as alleged concept of consciousness. If it is supposed to mean that it is a consciousness which has itself as an object, it presupposes that the consciousness which is the object is a consciousness having as its object something different from itself. Or else, as earlier mentioned, an infinite regress is inevitable. But if this is not what it is supposed to mean it is difficult, if not impossible, to see what it could mean. One thing is certain: A consciousness which is not a consciousness of something is not a consciousness at all.

However, if Fichte's philosophy is considered, not as an attempt at a description of the natural history or genesis of consciousness, but as an attempt at a description of its logical structure, it becomes clear that the concept of 'to posit' is not to be conceived of as a certain act performed at a certain point in history. Thus interpreted Fichte's philosophy, then, reads as follows. The infinite and absolute I (the transcendental apperception) is a necessary condition for consciousness and constitutes its (as well as its object's) unconditioned foundation. But there is no rule according to which the non-I can be deduced from the unconditioned and absolute I. The existence of the non-I does not follow by any necessity from the absolute I. To say that P is a necessary condition of Q does of course not entail the existence of Q. But if Q does exist the existence of P necessarily follows. And since consciousness as a matter of fact exists it does follow that the necessary conditions for consciousness are satisfied. All that one is entitled to read into Fichte's use of the concept of 'to posit' seems therefore only to be the negative assertion that the existence of that which is posited cannot be logically deduced from that which posits it. From the fact that the transcendental apperception is a necessary condition for consciousness it does not follow that there is any consciousness. The fact that there are language using beings does not follow from the condition for the existence of any language at all.

Even though the non-I is posited, and not a logical consequence of the I, it is, nevertheless, according to Fichte, crucial to ask why the I posits the non-I. In order to evaluate Fichte's answer it may be helpful to return to Kant. The concept of the **a priori** played a decisive part in Kant's philosophy. This concept he contrasted to the concept of the **a posteriori**. The latter concept constituted, so he thought, an inevitable element in all empirical knowledge. An essential element of empirical knowledge is that such knowledge is obtained only after experience has given its final accept. This is in contrast to knowledge which is a priori. A priori knowledge is not just prior to experience; it is totally independent of it. The validity of a priori knowledge can be neither verified nor falsified by experience. In writing his **Critique of Pure Reason** it was Kant's aim to discover the conditions of the a priori knowledge he thought we in fact possess. By the term 'pure' Kant means (in this connection) the logical structure of reason, i.e. the logical structure of reason as it is independent of any empirical content. The **Critique of Pure Reason** may thus be regarded as an investigation of reason as an instrument for attaining knowledge. The laws of nature are, according to Kant, fundamentally an expression of the structure of reason. In a certain sense, the laws of nature are dictated by reason. But, also according to Kant, it is not only the laws of nature which are dictated by the a priori structure of reason. Also morality is so dictated. Or to express it in Kantian terms: Reason has a theoretical as well as a practical aspect. Consequently, Kant wrote both his **Critique of Pure Reason** and his **Critique of Practical Reason**. Just as by necessity the different empirical laws of nature all reflect the a priori principles of reason, so human acts in order to be morally right must be motivated by the a priori moral law of reason, the law, namely, that the motive of every act performed must be that one can will that one's motive for the performed act could be a universal law.

Pure reason is thus dualistic. It is a dualism whose two aspects Kant did not succeed in bringing into a unity. Admittedly, in his third critique, **The Critique of Judgment**, Kant asserts that although the concept of causality is a category, i.e. a concept whose application is a condition for all experience, it nevertheless seems unquestionable or beyond dispute that there are phenomena where a causal explanation (an explanation through nothing but mechanical causes) appears to be insufficient. There are phenomena which seem to require an explanation in terms of a purpose, – require so-called teleological explanations. However, Kant is cautious in not drawing any metaphysical conclusions from this alleged fact. But he has no precautions concerning the moral law. A moral law, i.e. a law making demands. And the concept of a demand entails a demand for its fulfilment. Since, furthermore, it is a fact that both happiness as well as unhappiness exist, it would be contrary to the concept of morality if happiness were not bestowed upon those who deserved it; that is, bestowed upon those who had fulfilled the demands of the moral laws. In order to ensure a harmony between happiness and desert – a harmony by no means ensured by the laws of nature – a supreme being, i.e. God, is necessary. A connection between reason as practical and teleological and as theoretical is nowhere, however, to be found in Kant's philosophy.

In Fichte's philosophy such a connection is attempted. To the question why the absolute I posits itself as limiting, and at the same time as limited by, the posited non-I, the answer is as follows. The innermost essence of the unlimited and absolute I is of an ethical structure. An ethical act requires consciousness, and, accordingly, requires both the limited (and limiting) I as well as the limited (and limiting) non-I. Since the I through the non-I is confronted by its opposite it is confronted by a task, the task, namely, to realize itself as a potentially unlimited I. It is confronted with the task, therefore, to realize itself as an ethical being, which is the same as to realize one's freedom (the freedom that one is motivated by the a priori law constituting one's real self and, consequently, not motivated by something foreign, i.e. not motivated by the non-I). Since it is a goal that never can be reached it is a task requiring an infinite striving. If **per impossibili** the goal was obtained, it would imply that the limited I would have ceased to be limited; it would have completed the task of being the infinite and unlimited I. It would be a state without individuality and without consciousness. But such a paradoxical and self-destroying result is a conceptual impossibility: According to Fichte the essence of the absolute I is of an ethical nature which implies that the I must posit the limited I as well as the limited non-I. It is thus a necessity dictated by the nature or essence of the absolute I that there necessarily must be a limited I as well as a limited non-I.

To the question why the unlimited I posits the limited I and the limited non-I Fichte's answer is, then, that only thus is it possible that the unlimited I can realize itself as an ethical being. In other words, the metaphysical system justifies the ethical system. Practical philosophy enjoys priority over theoretical philosophy. Man, Fichte asserts, exists as a conscious being and a being endowed with reason in order to be able to actualize its potentiality as an ethical being, which is the same as to say that man exists as a conscious being and a being endowed with reason in order to be able to actualize its potentiality as a free being - free in the sense that only a being who is motivated by nothing but the a priori moral law is free. Only such a being is determined by itself and only such a being is free.

Schelling

To any gifted university student, at least in Germany during this period, i.e. the period whose philosophy this book is about, philosophy was of central significance - to some even a matter of life and death. And even though, as a matter of course, philosophers such as the Pre-Socratics, Plato, Aristotle, the Stoics, Spinoza, and Leibniz were studied it was the philosophy of Kant and Fichte which was of primary importance to study, discuss, and either accept or reject. There was a general agreement that a philosophical break-through was accomplished through Kant's philosophy; there was also a general agreement that the concept of the thing in itself was fatal to Kantianism. But whether Fichte's system represented the truth there could be, and was, disagreement about.

The young and brilliant Schelling began his philosophic career as an adherent of Fichte's philosophy. The task for philosophy (metaphysics) is, according to Schelling as it also was to Fichte, to find the foundation of knowledge - to find the unconditioned or the absolute. To search for the absolute, as did both Fichte and Schelling, is a Kantian influence. Although Kant consigned the absolute to be unobtainable and therefore a utopian ideal for all knowledge, it nevertheless constituted a necessary idea to Kantianism (necessary because it constituted the direction and goal for the ongoing strife of knowledge). But when Fichte and Schelling speak of the absolute they do so in a sense which is different from the sense in which Kant did.

The sense in which Fichte and Schelling speak about the absolute is that sense Kant accepted it as a reality. To Kant the

unconditioned condition for knowledge are two things: It is partly
the stuff of knowledge (the thing in itself), and partly the
transcendental apperception (the transcendental Ego). It is
against this duality that Fichte reacted: Kant's two unconditioned
conditions are mutually exclusive. Either one has to accept that
the unconditioned condition is the thing in itself (in other words,
one has to accept what Fichte calls dogmatism); or one has to
accept that the unconditioned condition is the transcendental Ego
(accept, therefore, idealism). As we have seen, Fichte chooses
idealism because, as he asserts, only those who submit to
spiritual enslavement choose dogmatism. Also Schelling chooses
idealism. And Schelling also (Fichte-like) emphasizes that the
unconditioned condition, the very foundation for all knowledge
and being, can be proven neither by logical deduction nor can it
be observed. If it could be proved by logical deduction it would
presuppose certain premises which, accordingly, would constitute
the condition for the alleged unconditioned. And if it could be
observed it would presuppose, as is the case with whatever
qualifies as a possible object of experience, that which one is
looking for: The foundation and condition for all knowledge and
experience. The foundation for all knowledge and experience
cannot itself be an instance of knowledge (because what, then,
would be the foundation of this particular instance of
knowledge?). Or expressed differently: Whatever qualifies as an
object for thinking and experience must by necessity be
conceptually determined. But since concepts, according to both
Fichte and Schelling, are rooted in the transcendental Ego - the
Ego which they regarded as the foundation and condition of all
knowledge, - it follows that it cannot itself be conceptually
determined. But even if it cannot be conceptually determined it
can be intuited in what Schelling, after Fichte, calls an
intellectual intuition.[22] It is doubtful, however, whether this
concept can be given a clear meaning - or any meaning at all.

What so to speak is intuited through the intellectual intuition is not the I as such (it would presuppose, as just mentioned, that it could be conceptually determined). What is intuited is the I in its intellectual act. In other words, the thinking of the I is object of the intellectual intuition. But this characterization of the intellectual intuition is dangerously close to circularity: The object of thinking as such is this very thinking. However, it is not quite what Schelling understands by intellectual intuition. An essential feature of the absolute, of the unconditioned, is its freedom; it is not - cannot be - characterized by anything else. It is self-determining and consequently free. Its essential feature is therefore what Schelling calls its transcendental freedom or simple and pure willing. This is the essential feature which is the unconditioned condition for self-consciousness and which is revealed through the intellectual intuition. In every instance of consciousness there is something of which one is conscious. In every instance of consciousness consciousness has an object. Schelling is well aware that the transcendental freedom cannot be the object of consciousness. Only conceptual disasters would result if the unconditioned condition for all consciousness should appear as an object of consciousness; and only conceptual disasters would result if the unconditioned condition for all employment of concepts should itself be conceptualized. And what cannot be conceptualized has trancended the limits of language and therefore also transcended, as many would assert, the limits of what can be given any meaning. What appears to be quite certain, however, is this: One difference between thinking (in the sense of pondering or speculating) and the physiological and biochemical processes in my organism is that thinking is self-determining which the organic processes are not. I choose and decide the objects of my thinking, but I do not choose or decide which organic processes should occur. By scientific investigations I may discover these processes, but I do not discover the content of my thinking by a scientific investigation.

I decide the objects of my day dreams (while, of course, I do not decide my dreams in my sleep), the thinking when I work, or my more or less witty conversational remarks. But I choose neither to have nor not to have the processes connected with my headaches or with the fact that my organism is aging. Admittedly, it does create difficulties to clarify how to understand the nature of this freedom. If Kant is right in his assertion that the concept of causality is a category, i.e. a concept whose employment is a necessary condition for all understanding, it follows that the transcendental freedom by conceptual necessity must remain inconceivable (not to say that it would be a meaningless concept). Today many would claim (and correctly so) that the way the concept of freedom is used according to ordinary language it poses no problem. Because according to the ordinary use of the concept of freedom it acquires its meaning by being the negation of a special kind of lack of freedom. A people has become free; it no longer lives under the unfreedom of the tyranny. A country has become free; it has obtained its own government, flag, etc.; its laws are no longer determined by the government of another country. The prisoner becomes free; he no longer suffers the unfreedom of the prison. The bachelor is free; he is not restricted by the rules of a marriage. But Schelling is not thinking of these kinds of freedom. He is thinking of the transcendental freedom, the will of the unconditioned condition. And, admittedly, it does constitute a problem to understand what it could mean to say that, in this transcendental sense, there was no freedom. If it is asserted that it was determined by something else it would then be a problem to understand what it could mean to say that this something else is unconditioned, and so on indefinitely. But as Schelling emphasizes, a necessary condition for having any knowledge at all is that there is an unconditioned condition; which is the same as to say that the absolute and, accordingly, the transcendental freedom exists.

In his works **On the Ego as Principle of Philosophy**, (Vom **Ich als Prinzip der Philosophie**, 1795), and **System of Transcendental Idealism**, (**System des Transzendentale Idealismus**, 1800), Schelling is highly influenced by Fichte's philosophy.[23] But already in **An Exposition of My System of Philosophy**, (**Darstellung meines Systems der Philosophie**, 1801), a significant difference between the philosophy of Fichte and Schelling had come into view. The central concept in the two mentioned works from respectively 1795 and 1800 is the concept of the I. In the work from 1801 it is the concept of reason. The change from 'I' to 'reason' is significant. Because even though the concept of the I as it was used by both Fichte and Schelling was not the individual or empirical I, but the universal I, it nevertheless cannot be exculpated from, in a logical sense, holding hands with the concept of subjectivity. By birth, i.e. in its original sense and, therefore, in its ordinary sense, the word 'I' is an expression of subjectivity. However justified the distinction between the empirical and subjective I and the universal I may well be, the very essence of the concept is destroyed if the subjective element is eliminated. This is not the case, however, so far as the concept of reason is concerned. Reason understood, not as the ability of the individual to act and to think rationally, but as universal reason, exists independently of the existence of rational beings.

An objection against this assertion would be the following: An essential feature of universal reason is necessity and universality. But only what can be true or false can meaningfully be said to have necessity. And only sentences used to make statements about reality, not reality itself, can be true or false.

In other words, it is only within a language that the concepts of necessity and unversality can be applied. And since language presupposes language using beings, it follows that it is conceptually impossible to apply the concept of reason independently of language using beings. One way to meet this objection would be as follows. If one accepts that there are categories, i.e. accepts that there are fundamental concepts constituting the necessary conditions for consciousness as such and, consequently, also for language as such, it follows that it must be the case that such conditions exist independently of the existence of that which is conditioned. No language can have emerged if the conditions for its emergence, for its coming to be (for its actualization as Aristotle would have said), had not already existed. They must have existed prior to and independent of that which they condition.

By positing reason instead of the I as the fundamental concept Schelling avoids what he terms Fichte's subjective idealism. The reason Schelling (and later Hegel) accuses Fichte of subjectivism is, of course, that the non-Ego is explained through the Ego. And, as already mentioned, that the essential, original, and ordinary meaning of the term 'I' is inseparable from subjectivism. But this inseparable conceptual tie between these two concepts, i.e. the concept 'I' and the concept 'subjectivity', has its root in the fact that the term 'I' originally and normally is used according to the individual, empirical and ordinary meaning. However, the I which posits the non-I is the universal I, i.e. an I which has nothing to do with subjectivism. In a sense the above mentioned essential meaning of the term I is negated when the term is no longer used in the individual sense but in the universal sense. The root for this meaning transcendence, for the jump from the individual to the universal, can be found in Kant who identifies the transcendental apperception – the transcendnetal unity of consciousness - with the transcendental Ego.

Nevertheless, one must be careful not to cut the tie between the individual I and the universal I. Because, as already mentioned, there are uses of the term which are rooted in the individual as well as the universal. It is the universal which so to speak is incarnated in the individual. If, for instance, I say that I answered him as politely as I could it is, partly, the universal I and partly the individual I. It is the universal I since it cannot be defined in terms of the empirical data (physiological and psychological) which constitute the individual and empirical I. It is the individual I since the sentence is uttered by and is referring to a particular person located in space and time. The I referred to in a sentence such as "I answered him as politely as I could" is thus a combination or a unity of the universal and the individual, or, if one prefers, the I possesses both an individual and a universal aspect. It is in this sense that it can be said that the individual I is an incarnation of the universal I.

The accusation of subjectivism launched against Fichte's system is considerably weakened by the above observations. It is, meanwhile, justifiable to criticize Fichte for a dialectical tension between the I and the non-I which characterizes his system. On the one hand, the non-I is precisely that which is opposite to and different from the I; the I and the non-I are two each other opposing worlds. On the other hand, the non-I is posited by the I; and that which is posited by the I cannot be radically opposed to it. It is a dialectical tension which, as earlier mentioned, corresponds to the tension between language and that which language is about. That which language is about is a non-linguistic reality and is, at the very same time, constituted by language and presupposes it.

By identifying all being, i.e. whatever is, with reason – identifying subjects and objects, consciousness and nature – does Schelling, then, overcome these conceptual difficulties? A great deal depends on what is to be understood by 'reason '. There is a straight line from Kant's transcendental apperception over Fichte to Schelling (and for that matter also to Hegel). The transcendental unity of consciousness is the foundation of absolute idealism. And to repeat once more: The transcendental unity of consciousness is not a psychological concept. It is not a concept which has been learned and verified through psychological experiments and observations. This it neither is nor could be, since the transcendental unity is the very presupposition for all consciousness – including psychological observations and experiments. Fichte's and Schelling's formula for this unity is 'I am I ', (Kant's "I think" that potentially or actually accompanies all my conscious acts). Which is the same as to say that the transcendental unity of consciousness implies self-consciousness. That self-consciousness, in order to avoid the infinite regress, also must involve consciousness of something different from itself, has been mentioned already, (I have consciousness of myself as a conscious I – an I which is conscious of itself as a conscious I, and so forth ad infinitum; in order to stop this endless series there will have to be something of which I am conscious and which is not an I conscious of itself). The all important point, however, is that the transcendental unity of consciousness is the necessary condition for the categories and their application. What Schelling must mean by reason, then, is the class of necessary conditions (the transcendental principles of reason) for all knowledge. And since Schelling asserts that nothing is outside reason it follows that these conditions determine whatever is - nature as well as consciousness. Reason permeates and displays itself in Being.

However, Schelling means something more by reason. As already mentioned, in his **Critique of Judgment**, cautiously and almost with a bad conscience, Kant thought it necessary to find a place for final or teleological explanations. For an adequate understanding of nature, purposes, he thought, were unavoidable. And without a bad conscience Fichte had the I posit both itself as well as the non-I in order that the moral will could be actualized and therefore also freedom be actualized. To Schelling the teleological conception is essential. How in the last analysis Schelling conceived the purpose shall later be explained. At present it suffices to mention what appears to be trivially true, although it is not quite so trivial in reality, namely this: The function (i.e. the purpose) of reason must, according to its very nature, be to understand and to explain. The concept of reason is a teleological concept.

When Schelling maintains that he is not a subjectivist (as he maintains that Fichte is) it, therefore, seems that it is more verbally than substantially that his idealism is more objective than Fichte's idealism. To the extent that it is justified to accuse Fichte's idealism of being a subjective form of idealism to that extent it is justified to accuse Schelling's idealism of being an expression of subjectivism. But as I have argued, it is by overlooking or ignoring that the I which is the foundation of Fichte's idealism is, not the individual or empirical, but the absolute and universal I that one is led to the view that Fichte is a subjectivist. Moreover, since Schelling's concept of reason is an expression of, inter alia, self-consciousness, or rather the condition of self-consciousness (formulated through the formula 'I am I') he can, for the same reason - or lack of reason, - be called a subjectivist.

Schelling avoids, however, what Fichte did not avoid, the dialectical tension between the subject and its object - in the language of Fichte's philosophy, between the I and the non-I, or in Schelling's language, between nature and consciousness (or spirit). Nothing exists over and above reason. Nature is accordingly the visible reason. Reason is displayed in nature. Reason shows its face in nature.

Before this point is further developed it is necessary to emphasize that there is nothing which could be called Schelling's philosophic system as such, at least not in the sense according to which it is justifiable to talk about Kant's, Fichte's, and, especially, Hegel's systems. As the brilliant, vivacious, and restless mind he was, Schelling could not adhere to a once and for all worked out system. However, there are certain fundamental views through which Schelling's philosophy can be identified. The 'I ', as we have just seen, was replaced by the concept of reason, and this concept was later replaced by the concept of the Absolute and the Spirit; through this conceptual development the way was cleared for the theory of identity which is Schelling's most important contribution to absolute idealism - a contribution which by and large, at least so far as the essential elements are concerned, was adopted by Hegel. It is due to the theory of identity that Schelling is able to avoid the dialectical tension between subject and object.

The essential elements of the identity theory has already been mentioned: Reason (the Absolute, the Spirit) is everything and outside reason nothing is. Both nature and consciousness are thus a display of reason. Nature and consciousness therefore have the same rational structure. In other words, there is identity between nature and consciousness. Nature is the visible reason (spirit) and reason (spirit) is the invisible nature. But reason, in the way it manifests itself in nature (the visible but

unconscious reason), has as its purpose - has as its teleological
determination - to become the invisible but conscious reason. Or
expressed differently: The aim of reason is to be conscious of
itself. It is an essential part of the concept of reason that its aim
is to understand; and if reason is everything and there is
nothing outside reason it follows that the aim must be self-
understanding, that is, self-consciousness. Nature obtains
knowledge of itself; reason regards nature as its own
objectification. Nature constitutes the object for the subject, but
through reason it is understood that the object is identical with
the subject. Schelling here expresses the reaction of the romantic
concept of the philosophy of nature against the Cartesian dualism.
According to this dualism there is the extended but not thinking
substance (**res extensa**), and the unextended but thinking
substance (**res cogitans**). When Schelling speaks about the Spirit
in Nature he does not speak about two different substances; he
does not speak about a **res extensa** and a **res cogitans** which
are emerged in each other. The expression 'the Spirit in Nature'
must be understood in analogy with the spiritual (rational)
nature, i.e. as an adjective to 'nature'. It is consequently not to
be regarded as (to use an expression from present day
philosophical jargon) a "Ghost in the machine". According to the
Cartesian view, nature is not an expression of reason but is
thought, rather, in analogy with a machine, i.e. as a mechanical
system. The one exception is man who besides a body (a
mechanical system) possesses a soul, a **res cogitans**.

Schelling does not regard nature as a machine. Nature
cannot be explained and understood as a mechanical system.
Nature is not just a substance ontologically different from
consciousness and spirit. There is no metaphysical gap but a
continuous transition between nature and consciousness; this
continuous transition Schelling interprets as the drive inherent in

nature toward consciousness of itself. When nature, via human
consciousness, has arrived at this goal it understands that its
object is itself. Human consciousness is the eye through which
nature sees and understands itself. According to the mechanical
conception of nature, asserted and developed by, e.g., Hobbes,
Descartes, and Newton, nature is understood exclusively by help
of mechanical forces; according to Schelling nature can be
understood only as the not yet conscious spirit.

To regard nature as an expression of reason involves a
teleological view, i.e. a view according to which the ultimate
principle for all explanations is in terms of purposes. Schelling's
teleological system must not be mistaken for the teleological
system we tend to accept when we explain, for instance,
biological or physiological processes. Schelling's concern is to
show how the development from the lowest forms of existence
(i.e. the lowest in the series beginning with the inorganic and
ending with self-consciousness) to the higher forms can be
explained by referring to the ultimate purpose, i.e. the self-
consciousness of nature. Each step is explained as the
presupposition for the next one, and not as the effect of the
preceding one.

The difference between Fichte and Schelling with respect to
the subject-object relation is thus this. The dialectical tension
which in Fichte's system characterizes the relation between subject
and object - between the I and the non-I, - becomes in
Schelling's system a relation of identity.

The highest form of knowledge - absolute knowledge - is to
have understood the presupposition of all explanations; it is to
have knowledge of the absolute. It is to have understood that
subject and object are expressions of one and the same absolute
reason. To have obtained absolute knowledge - or as Schelling

also expresses it: To have knowledge of the Absolute, - is to have understood that, in Schelling's words, there is indifference between subject and object. Or in other words, in the absolute there are neither subjects nor objects.

That the absolute must be indifferent with respect to subjects and objects follows furthermore from the view that absolute reason, or the absolute, unfolds itself in nature as well as in consciousness. And since nature is the unconscious reason and the distinction between subject and object is applicable to consciousness only, it follows that absolute reason, or the absolute, is indifferent with respect to subject and object. Since furthermore reason, or the absolute, constitutes whatever is - constitutes whatever has being - it follows that no subject-object judgment can be passed. Any subject-object judgment must, according to the logic of the concept of such judgments, express limitation of that which the judgment is about. If I say: "The flower is yellow," I have said very little about the flower. The knowledge expressed through that judgment is very limited. If I knew everything there is to know (i.e. if I had infinite knowledge), I could say infinitely many things. Knowledge of the flower involves botany, which in turn involves chemistry and physics, which, ultimately, rests on principles of metaphysics. That principles of metaphysics are involved follows from the simple fact that the different sciences, e.g. physics, in the last analysis, cannot help encountering the problems of the nature of the objects of experience. That is, the physicist, for instance, to the extent that he intends to have full understanding of his science must understand the problems to which such metaphysical views as materialism, phenomenalism, realism, and idealism are the attempted answers. A full understanding and knowledge of an individual object thus involves understanding and knowledge of everything. It would involve an understanding and knowledge of the absolute and infinite reason. Or expressed differently, it would involve the self-understanding and self-knowledge of the absolute and infinite reason. But this kind of understanding and knowledge cannot be expressed as a subject-object judgment; it can be expressed only as the judgment 'A is A.', or in the language of idealism 'I am I'. Such a judgment has a logic quite different from a subject-object judgment. As we have seen, the judgment 'I am I' cannot be an expression of consciousness in the sense in which consciousness entails someone being conscious of something; if it were it would involve an infinite regress and thus be self-refuting. Consciousness in this sense of consciousness can be expressed only as a subject-object judgment, i.e. as a judgment which expresses a limited knowledge.

Schelling's concept of the infinite or absolute reason - the concept of that which constitutes the ontological as well as the epistemological foundation, - is, paradoxically, thus outside all knowledge. It is condemned to eternal epistemological darkness. Which it must be, of course, as long as it is conceived the way Kant, Fichte, and Schelling conceived it. The unconditioned foundation for all being and knowledge must by necessity itself be something unexplained and unknowable. To Kant the stuff and therefore the foundation for all knowledge and experience, was, according to his epistemological principles, excluded for ever from becoming an object of knowledge. And, as we have seen, the very assumption of the existence of the concept of the stuff, i.e. the thing in itself, carries with it a contradiction.

Fichte, whose philosophical system had the avoidance of this contradiction as its purpose, realized that his infinite and absolute I, precisely because it constituted the foundation of knowledge and experience, could not possibly be an object for knowledge either. Instead he introduced the concept of 'intellectual intuition' by which he understood an immediate

consciousness of the acting I and immediate consciousness of
which act the I is performing. Expressed negatively: The
knowledge one possesses of one's own acts is obtained neither
through experience nor by an inference, (it is a kind of
knowledge which is non-empirical and non-derivative). What
Fichte calls intellectual intuition is in fact identical with the
modern concept of intention; the concept of intention is
conceptually tied to the concept of an act and is characterized by
just such features which, according to Fichte, characterizes the
intellectual intuition.[24] As Wittgenstein says: The element of
surprise is lacking. But even if Fichte's concept of intellectual
intuition is adequate it informs only (informs in a non-empirical
and non-inferential way) that I perform this particular act, but it
does not inform anything about (which is a transcendental
impossibility) the Nature of the Ego except that it is an acting
Ego, or as Schelling says, an Ego endowed with a will.

But although Schelling has to admit that the absolute -
absolute reason - transcends the limits of knowledge, he all the
same thinks that the artistic genius through his artistic creativity
reveals the absolute. An art work is in itself a finite and limited
empirical object; it is an objectification of the absolute. In a
work of art the infinite is revealed in the finite, the freedom of
the spirit in the necessity of laws of nature, the universal in the
particular.[25]

Through this theory Schelling has transcended the border of
metaphysics as a philosophic discipline and moved into the poetic-
romantic area. The artist himself has no consciousness or
knowledge of what the absolute is. Although the **work** of art he
has created is an action of which he is conscious, the specifically
artistic - i.e. that the infinite and the universal are revealed in
his creation - is something of which he is not conscious. He is
ignorant of being an instrument employed by the absolute (the

infinite and absolute reason or spirit) to the purpose of revealing the absolute through the finite and the particular. Through his artistic creation the artist unknowingly transcends his own limited and finite existence.

Schelling's philosophy thus concludes by negating itself. To have to conclude that the goal of his philosophy (i.e., to find the absolute, to find the foundation of being, consciousness, and knowledge) is inattainable because it transcends the limits of knowledge, is not only a negation of philosophic thought; it is to accept a concept (the absolute) whose meaning, if it indeed has any meaning at all, may very well be doubted. It is important, therefore, to ask the question if, and if so then where in his system, Schelling takes the fateful step which leads him to the metaphysical misere.

It is not in itself necessarily a fault of a philosophical system to arrive at the conclusion that the ground of all being is unknowable. But to a system which maintains that reason is everything and that besides reason there is nothing, it comes close to a paradox to assert that reason (the absolute or spirit) is outside the reach of knowledge. Because whatever may be meant by the concept of reason it does appear to be a contradiction to assert that reason in itself is unknowable and incomprehensible.

It seems obvious, however, that if a system is based on a conceptual model according to which all understanding and explanation presuppose a single concept or principle - be it the Kantian concept of the thing in itself, Fichte's absolute Ego, or Schelling's absolute reason, - then, by necessity, such a concept or principle is outside what can be understood and experienced. Schelling was within an edge of avoiding the paradox. He sees that reason cannot be the cause of being (such as, for instance,

Fichte's absolute Ego was). Reason, so he claims, is not the cause of the universe - it is the universe.[26] If he had analyzed the concept of reason more deeply, he would have been able to free himself from the conceptual model in which he was imprisoned. Hegel succeeded in freeing himself from this model - the Hegel who in many respects (more so than it is generally recognized) owed to Schelling his philosophic break-through. According to Hegel it is not a single or a particular principle which constitutes the presupposition for the system. To Hegel the absolute or universal reason is the very process (the dialectical process), which constitutes the essence of reason. The logical structure of the dialectical process is described and explained in Hegel's **Logic** - primarily in his **Science of Logic**. His **Science of Logic** is accordingly a description and explanation of the absolute or, as Hegel also says, of God. His logic is a description of the essence of God. It is a description of God's essence before creation.

When the collapse of Schelling's philosophy is emphasized its merits ought also to be emphasized. It was a significant step when Schelling perceived nature, as he said, as the visible spirit and consciousness as the invisible nature. The difficulty in connection with the subject-object relation, the way it was conceived according to Fichte's philosophy was that his non-Ego, despite the fact that it was posited by the Ego, remained non-Ego. In Schelling's philosophy Fichte's non-Ego became nature, i.e. a nature in which reason unfolds. From nature (the visible but fossilized spirit) to spirit (the invisible nature), there was no unbridgeable gulf but a continuous transition. It is unnecessary, in this place, to dwell upon or discuss whether Schelling through his conceptual scheme conceived the transition from one particular level in nature to the next, or from nature to consciousness, as a process, i.e. a process through which absolute reason unfolded and developed itself with the purpose of obtaining self-consciousness. It appears as if he let the question remain unanswered as he at the same time admitted as a possibility that it was in fact a process. But what he did not regard as a mere possibility but regarded as a fact, was that both nature in all its different levels as well as consciousness were an expression of absolute reason. Nature was the arena in which reason was revealed.

If Schelling's language appears offensive - a language using expressions such as absolute reason, spirit in nature, and several others (and, admittedly, to a person trained in and accustomed to the language of the sciences and philosophy of today such expressions must seem not only unusual but also rather provoking),- then the all important problem necessary to solve should not be forgotten. It is a problem which neither Hume nor Kant nor Fichte had been able to solve. Each of these philosophers radicalized, not to say revolutionized, his predecessor's view. Kantianism overcame the inadequacy, not to say the impotence, of Hume's philosophy, but the price Kantianism had to pay was the contradictory concept of the thing in itself - a concept Fichte overcame, but overcame only by accepting the above mentioned dialectical tension between the Ego and the non-Ego. It is this tension Schelling attempts to ease. The philosophic advance from Hume's philosophy has thus been achieved by each philosopher radicalizing his predecessor's conceptual scheme.

Let me now try to recast Schelling's form of absolute idealism as a problem about language and the object of language. That language requires a non-linguistic reality as an object has been mentioned several times in the preceding pages. It has also been mentioned and explained how the relation between language and its object is pregnant with dialectical problems. Somewhat simplified it is possible to describe the dialectic in the following way. According to the first step, the non-linguistic reality (e.g. Hume's sense impressions) are independent of language in so far as existence as well as structure are concerned. The transition to the second step was necessitated by the fact that the necessary conditions for having any language at all were incompatible with the view characterizing the first step. The insight that the non-linguistic reality, although independent of language so far as existence is concerned, did depend on language so far as its structure is concerned characterizes the second step. It does so because structure is determined by the a priori conditions of language - the conditions it was impossible to satisfy in the first step, and consequently, necessitated that the first step had to be given up.

According to the third step the non-linguistic reality is dependent on language so far as existence as well as structure are concerned. From enjoying logical priority over language in the first step, the non-linguistic reality becomes, in the third step, secondary in relation to language. Without a language nothing would be. Nothing exists or occurs if it cannot be conceptually determined; it consequently follows that without a conceptual apparatus, without a language (not this or that particular language, but language as such, that is, language in its platonic existence) there is no reality; to exist without existing as something is not to exist at all. It is to exist just as little as the Kantian thing in itself is an existing thing.

The third step was arrived at due to the fact that the second step (the Kantian philosophy) involved the concept of a non-linguistic reality existing independently of language, - a feature which implies, as we have seen, a contradiction. To assume the existence of a non-linguistic reality which is independent of language implies the application of concepts and categories. But such an application contradicts the assumption that the reality to which they are applied is a non-linguistic reality. However, even if the elimination of this contradictory concept was achieved through the third step, a problem remained, the problem, namely, corresponding to the dialectical tension in Fichte's philosophy between the Ego and the non-Ego. The non-Ego is posited by the Ego in order that the Ego can have an object - if there were no object for the Ego there would not be any Ego. Corresponding to the relation between the Ego and the non-Ego is the relation between a language and the non-linguistic reality. The non-linguistic reality is 'posited' by language in order that language can be a language. The non-linguistic reality is a necessary condition for the existence of language. But how can the non-linguistic reality be of a non-linguistic nature if it is posited by language? Not only is language a presupposition for its existence; it is in itself a linguistic entity in so far as it cannot be conceived, assumed as existing, or thought but for the categories of language.

The dualism between language and the non-linguistic reality (betwen the Ego and the non-Ego) has not been overcome at the third step; the non-linguistic reality is of a linguistic as well as of a non-linguistic nature. The logical structure of the non-linguistic reality is thus a reflection of the logical structure of language as it at the same time is not of such a structure. This has been overcome through the fourth step (that is, through Schelling's philosophic system). The logical structure of the non-linguistic reality is not a reflection of the logical structure of language. Neither of them is a reflection of the other. The logical structure one finds in the non-linguistic reality one also finds in language without the one being the cause of the other and without one enjoying logical priority over the other. Language as well as the non-linguistic reality are both an unfolding of the same logical structure, or expressed differently, of one and the same rationality.

An example may illustrate this point. Suppose I say that a billiard ball is pushing another billiard ball, or that I cut something with a knife. The logic of the verb 'to push' implies that the object pushed receives an impulse to be moved in the direction of the push, just as the logic of the verb 'to cut' implies that the thing on which I use the knife will be cut. It follows from the logic which is built into these verbs. The logic resides in language and not in that which language is about. The home of logic, so it might be asserted, is the I or consciousness (language), and not the object (the non-linguistic reality). But according to Schelling's philosophy (the fourth step) it is not just because the logic is built into the verb 'to push' and the verb 'to cut' that it follows by necessity that the object pushed or the object which one attempts to cut, is pushed (in the sense that it receives an impulse to move in the push's direction) or cut (in the sense that it will be cut unless the object to be cut is too hard or the knife is too dull),[27] - it is also because it is part of the logic of the non-linguistic reality. There is no possibility of conceiving that something is pushing something or that something is being cut in any other way than by help of the concepts of 'to push' and 'to cut'. Admittedly, a being who possesses no concepts (i.e., a being who does not use a language) does not conceive of the necessity of the occurrences. Such a being (e.g. an animal) does not do this for the simple reason that it has no consciousness of what occurs (there is no consciousness of - there cannot be - a **whatness**). But when a language has developed, the rationality of the non-linguistic reality is, via language, understood. It is not the case that the logic of language is read into the non-linguistic reality, but it is through language that one acquires knowledge of the logic of the non-

linguistic reality. The calamity of the fourth step is that the
rationality, which is conceived in whatever is and which is the
supposed foundation of all explanation and understanding, itself
transcends knowledge and understanding. This calamity is one of
the points which is criticized by Hegel. As already mentioned,
only by conceiving the absolute foundation of understanding and
explanation, not as the socle upon which the column rests, but as
the dialectical process in itself, was it possible for Hegel to avoid
the calamity of the fourth step.

Hegel

The Preface

Among the creators of absolute Idealism the best known, at least outside the world of professional philosophers, is Hegel. In a way Hegel finished what Kant, Fichte and Schelling had begun. Schelling, as we have seen, changed Fichte's non-rational non-Ego into rational nature (the fossilized spirit); at the same time, however, he relegated universal reason - the Absolute - to epistemological darkness. Since universal reason or the Absolute by Schelling was asserted to be, not the cause of being but identical with it, it is the same as to assert that being is outside all possible knowledge: Being transcends the limits of knowledge. Hegel's contribution is to redeem universal reason or the Absolute from the imprisonment of ignorance. According to Hegel not only could the Absolute be known - not only be regarded as the highest kind of knowledge, - it occupied its rightful place as the knowledge without which there could be no knowledge at all.

It has been said that Hegel is more influenced by Plato and Aristotle than by Kant, Fichte and Schelling.[28] But this is misleading. Hegel was, of course, influenced by all the great philosophers of the past, not least by Plato and Aristotle. But the problems which mostly occupied his mind he inherited from neither Plato nor Aristotle, nor from Spinoza or Leibniz. The metaphysical problems confronting and occupying Hegel and his contemporary fellow-philosophers were primarily the unsolved problems and puzzles of Kant and Fichte. It was Kant's and

Fichte's problems which created the philosophic background for Hegel's **Phenomenology.** Kant's and Fichte's problems were also Hegel's problems, although neither Kant's nor Fichte's solutions were Hegel's solutions. Yet even this assertion is misleading. Because the problems in question are independent of time, culture and geography. They are inherent in reason itself. They are universal. They are constitutive of the dialectical logic of the fundamental metaphysical concepts. They constitute in fact the fundamental problem of metaphysics. The problem about the logical and ontological status of the object of consciousness - and this is what the problem basically is about - constitutes by necessity a problem. To the non-philosophic mind it does not, of course, constitute a problem. The non-philosophic view may be characterized as naive-realism. But through the insight that the known object, by being known, is submitted to the conditions of knowledge (i.e. to the categories) the Kantian problem is inescapable. Inescapable is it also, that philosophy has to advance beyond Kantian philosophy. Philosophy cannot rest at Kantianism with its contradictory concept of the thing in itself, - i.e. a philosophy which at the same time it presupposes the existence of an independent reality it also cannot conceive of such a reality except in terms which negate its alleged independence. As we have seen, Fichte attempted to repair Kantianism, as Schelling in turn attempted to improve Fichte's philosophy. And finally Hegel attempts to rectify the defects of Schelling's philosophy. But even though the problem is necessary (and therefore timeless) then only through Kant did philosophy reach the maturity required in order that the problem became a problem to human thought.

Two possible objections should be mentioned. The first one is that it is incorrect to maintain that the problem did not arise before the arrival of Kantianism. To Locke and Descartes for instance, the problem is whether the external world in itself possesses only the primary qualities; or, rather, it is asserted that secondary qualities are not qualities which the object in itself possesses. But the arguments for such a view are more physiological of nature than they are philosophical. The arguments rely on certain physiological theories of how in fact perceptions take place, i.e. how they are conditioned by the structure and function of the sense-organs and by theories of optics. It does not possess, therefore, the conceptual necessity which characterizes a philosophical theory.

The second objection is this. The problem of the nature of the object of consciousness is, so the objection goes, a problem for the natural sciences to solve and therefore not a philosophical problem. Is it not the case that quantum theory, for instance,[29] has more or less revolutionized our common sense notion of the objective world? But nor is this objection relevant. However interesting and however true quantum theory may be it is not - cannot be - a theory of the necessary conditions of experience and knowledge. It is not - cannot be - an investigation of the logic of the basic concepts which constitute the necessary conditions for having any experience and knowledge at all, and consequently also constitute the necessary conditions for quantum theory. No scientific theory can be a theory about the conditions for the existence of itself. It may be objected, furthermore, that although it may be correct that for instance Locke's theory and theories of the natural sciences such as quantum theory do not qualify as philosophic theories offered in order to solve philosophic problems, it is different with respect to a theory such as Democritus' atomic theory. Admittedly, Democritus did not base his theory on observations or experiments. Whether his theory should be classified as a scientific theory advanced in order to solve the philosophic problem associated with the concept of change, or it should be classified as a philosophical theory, may

be debated.   But even though the problem of change is a
philosophic problem it is not the problem Idealism is concerned
about.   Moreover, and this is essential, Democritus' theory is
secondary in relation to the problem of Idealism. The problem of
Idealism is a presupposition for the atomic theory in as much as
Democritus in his theory presupposes that the world consists of
corporeal   particles,   i.e.,   of   extended   matter,   which   exist
independently   of   consciousness   and   independently   of   the
conditions of knowledge.

Hegel who matured more slowly than did Schelling, his junior
by four years, had reached the age of 37 (i.e. the year 1807)
when he published one of his most important works. It was a
work which came to exert great influence upon the development of
philosophy.   The title of the work is **Phenomenology of Spirit,**
(Die Phänomenologie des Geistes).[30] As so many of the works
of great distinction within philosophy it is a very difficult work
to read.   However, since it is a work of fundamental significance
for the understanding of Hegel's philosophy it is important to
study it. It is hardly an exaggeration to say, what has often
been said, that the **Phenomenology** is the most original, the most
brilliant, the most important, and the most interesting of Hegel's
works.

The **Phenomenology** has a long preface (all of Hegel's books
have prefaces, many of which are unusually long); it is a preface
which, due to its virtues as well as to its unvirtuous, or at least
not so virtuous, difficulties has acquired a special place in the
history of philosophy. The verdict has been passed that not only
is it the most important chapter of the **Phenomenology** but also
the most important pages Hegel ever wrote. On this point
Hermann Glockner (editor of **Die Jubiläumsausgabe**) says:
"Whoever has understood the Preface to the **Phenomenology** has
understood Hegel."[31]   One is tempted to add: "And whoever has

not understood it does not understand Hegel." The Preface is difficult to understand. This it is for the following reasons. The Preface presupposes that the reader is well acquainted with the problems which constituted the philosophical milieu in which Hegel and his time's philosophers were educated. It furthermore presupposes (or almost presupposes) that the reader has read the **Phenomenology.** Hegel wrote the Preface after having finished the manuscript; that is, he wrote it after he had worked his way through the problems. It is, from a psychological point of view, understandable that an author, who over a longer period of time has worked with, speculated and thought of the problems and found his way through them, is apt to forget that the reader does not have the same familiarity with these problems and arguments. All of which is an argument for reading the Preface as the last thing of the **Phenomenology** and not, as would be the logical thing to do, as the first thing. Another reason for the difficulties in reading the Preface is Hegel's style. Although Hegel wrote with considerable literary style he did not write in a popular way. This he did not do as little as did, e.g., Kant. One did not write philosophy for anybody. Besides, in Hegel's time philosophic education and knowledge were more common within the academic world than it is today.

The Preface (in the Meisner edition) is 50 pages. A detailed examination of it cannot be given here. However, in the following pages some of its most important points shall be mentioned.

The Preface begins by asserting a view which is central to Hegelianism. Although it is customary, so Hegel says, that an author in the preface to a literary work explains the aim of the work and explains the relation between his own views and the views of other authors it is misplaced so far as a philosophical work is concerned; it would be particularly misplaced or misleading if it was taken to imply that the author's view represents the truth and that, consequently, all other views are false. The reason Hegel opposes such a view is his assumption that every philosophic system is an expression of an aspect or part of the truth. Although no philosophic system of the past expresses the whole truth they all express a part or some aspect of it. Truth is the fruit of universal reason. Truth is the fruit, therefore, of a philosophic system. Which amounts to saying that the history of philosophy reveals the dialectical development of truth. Each moment in this development presupposes the preceding moment and is itself a presupposition of the succeeding one. The fact that two philosophical systems are different does consequently not imply that one (or at least one) is false. Instead of seeing two philosophic systems as two entirely different systems in the sense that if the one is true the other must by necessity be false - instead of seeing them as two systems which contradict each other, - they ought to be seen as two systems where the differences between them express different moments of the dialectical development of the truth. Hegel illustrates this in the following way. The blossom is preceded by the bud. When the bud bursts the blossom comes out, and, finally, after the blossom comes the fruit. According to the view Hegel opposes, the bud, the blossom, and the fruit correspond to three each other contradicting philosophic systems and where only, at most, one of them can represent the truth and the two others, if not all three, are false. What Hegel asserts is that none of them are false. Each of them is a presupposition for the succeeding one. An essential part of what is meant by a bud is that it is a necessary and last step before the development of the blossom; it is what by botanical necessity precedes the existence of the blossom just as what is meant by a fruit, at least in part, is what necessarily is preceded by the blossom. The three existent entities cannot be isolated from each other: together they constitute a whole. To regard the blossom, for instance, as a falsification of the bud would obviously be an expression of lack of understanding. If the fruit is regarded as an isolated entity the blossom as well as the bud must consequently be regarded as false. But if the bud, the blossom, and the fruit are regarded as a whole, it follows that although the three entities are incompatible and cannot possibly exist at one and the same time they nevertheless constitute a whole or a unit in the sense that each step - each moment - is a necessary condition for the succeeding one. In order to understand the nature of the fruit it is necessary to understand the nature of the blossom and the bud. It is necessary to understand how the fruit has developed from the blossom and how the blossom has developed from the bud. To understand the fruit is to understand its becoming.

The aim of philosophy is, accordingly, not just a description, a statement, or an expression of the result of the philosophizing. That it is as little as the aim of botany is nothing over and above a description of the fruit. To botany it is the description of the result in connection with the process leading to the result which is of importance. The same is true of philosophy. To philosophy too it is the result in connection with the philosophizing process which leads to the result that matters. Or expressed differently: An explanation and an understanding of the result involves concepts which themselves can be understood only by the help of concepts used for the construction of the philosophic system. Truth can be found, therefore, only in and through a fully worked out system. To say that truth can be found in and through a philosophic system is the same as to say that it could be found in and through a conceptual system. But such a dictum can hardly be said to be revolutionary. Because on what other grounds could anything claim to represent the truth except through compelling arguments. Any truth-claim can

be made only on the presentation of sufficient evidence. Nothing
can qualify as an argument unless the logic of the involved
concepts is mastered; and nothing can be experienced or
observed unless it is experienced and observed by help of the
relevant concepts which determine **what** it is that is experienced
or observed, i.e. determine its whatness, (if that which is
experienced cannot be determined as something, nothing is
determined or observed). But even if Hegel's dictum hardly can
be said to be revolutionary it should not be forgotten (and Hegel
did not forget) that according to Schelling truth (the truth about
the absolute) could not be obtained through philosophic thought,
i.e. could not be found in or through a philosophic system; to
Schelling the truth about the absolute could be revealed only
through artistic creation. Hegel does not mention Schelling by
name, but that he has Schelling in mind is a historical fact.

Hegel also criticizes Schelling, again without mentioning his
name, by ridiculing the view (held by Schelling) that in the
absolute there is no difference between subject and object.
Everything, then, becomes identical with everything else. It is,
Hegel says, like the night in which every cow is black.

In an often quoted statement Hegel says: "The True is thus
the Bacchanalian revel in which no member is not drunk; yet
because each member collapses as soon as he drops out, the revel
is just as much transparent and simple repose."[32] At first this
statement seems to contradict the statement that truth exists only
in the philosophic system (whether Hegel's system or the systems
of any of his predecessors). And this very statement is itself
obviously regarded as being absolutely true. But the truths
which collapse and drop out, i.e. the truths that are like the
Bacchanalian revel, are the truths of the particular moments of
the dialectical process. The bud as an instance ("truth") of the
botanic reality ceases as an existing instance as soon as the

blossom becomes reality. The bud as such participates in the Bacchanalian revel. But the truth of the botanical system - the system which describes, explains, and due to which it is understood how the blossom succeeds the bud - is not itself a member of the Bacchanalian revel. Expressed differently: The truth of the above quoted statement according to which the truth is said to be a member of the Bacchanalian revel cannot itself be a member of this revel - it can be this as little as can all the alleged true statements of the **Phenomenology** (or the alleged truth of the **Phenomenology** as such).

Since the relation between subject and object is of central significance for Absolute Idealism it is important to examine the Hegelian view. In fact Hegel's view of this relationship is a decisive expression of his philosophy. In one of the most important statements of the Preface Hegel says: "In my view, which can be justified only by the exposition of the system itself, everything turns on grasping and expressing the True not only as Substance but equally as Subject."[33]

To say as Hegel does in the just quoted passage, that everything turns on this view is, as already mentioned, to allot a central, or even the most central, place to it. And as Hegel also says, the view can be justified only through the exposition of the system - which is in accordance with the earlier mentioned statement, that the truth is neither the result nor the process which leads to the result, but is the result comprehended as a result of the process. Or as Hegel expresses it, the truth is the fruit in so far as it is understood as an end-product of a process which began at the bud. Although the **Phenomenology** contains many philosophical reflections and philosophic arguments which are not directly relevant to the assertion about the identity between subject and substance, the arguments for this identity and the description of the dialectical process leading to it as well

as analysis of it constitute the essential aim of the
Phenomenology. It is what the **Phenomenology** in the last
analysis is about.

Hegel's identification of subject and substance or, which is
the same, subject and object, is an identification which is
actualized when the subject has actualized itself as object or
substance, i.e. has objectivized or universalized itself.[34]

It is a universalization or an objectivization which is
actualized through a rational, or, better, a philosophical process.
It is a process of which Hegel's **Phenomenology** is a description.
When Hegel speaks of the subject he has in mind, as had his
predecessors, neither the empirical nor the individual subject,
but the universal subject. It is thus an identity between the
knowing or comprehending universal subject and the object known
or comprehended which is asserted. And if by the knowing or
comprehending subject is meant the general and universal rules
and principles of knowledge (i.e. that which remains when
whatever is empirical and individual is subtracted), then it is in
accordance with the earlier given (cf. p.59) characterization of
Absolute Idealism, the characterization, namely, that the general
and universal principles of consciousness and knowledge (or, if
one prefers, the categories or logical conditions of language)
constitute the conditions of the existence of the substance or the
object.

The dialectical process leading to the understanding and
knowledge of this identity is a historical process - a process
described and explained through the history of philosophy. It is
a process through which the universal subject - via or through
the individual consciousness (the universal subject, it will be
remembered, is a subject without consciousness; consciousness is
actualized only as an empirical or individual consciousness), -

actualizes the understanding and knowledge of the identity. It is a process leading from the not yet known and understood, although existing, identity (in Hegel's terms it exists **"an sich"** - exists in itself) to the actualized knowledge and understanding of it (it then exists not merely **"an sich"** but **"an und für sich"** - exists in itself and for itself).

Let me once more emphasize the cardinal difference between Hegel and his predecessors. To Fichte and Schelling the Absolute had an existence independent of the philosophic thinking, independent of the dialectical process, leading to the Absolute. The path leading to the Absolute was not identical with the Absolute. The Absolute was the pedestal on which all knowledge and understanding had to rest; it is the presupposition of all knowledge; and as a presupposition of all knowledge it cannot itself be an object of knowledge. According to Hegel, however, the Absolute is not distinct from philosophic thought. The Absolute is identical with the philosophic system - identical with the system from its beginning to its end. In a philosophic system which, through the dialectical process of its philosophic arguments, shows that there is identity between subject and object, the Absolute is not a night in which all cows are black. It is the very system which shows (or proves) that there is such an identity. The Absolute is the completed system; it is the dialectical process as well as its result. Hegel's Absolute is thus an Absolute which **par excellence** can be an object of knowledge.

The development from the potentially known (that which exists **"an sich"**) to the actually known (that which exists **"an und für sich"**) should not be regarded as a psychological development or process. The description of the development is not a description of how the obtained knowledge is in fact, step by step, obtained. The **Phenomenology** is a philosophic treatise; it is not a psychological one. The development is not explainable in

terms of psychological laws; it is explainable in terms of the logic
of the relevant concepts.

Against this view the following objection may be forwarded:
How is it possible that the dialectical process may be claimed to
be understood as a process determined, not by contingent and
through observation falsifiable laws, but by the logic of the
relevant concepts? The objection or, rather the question, is not
unlike (but surely not identical with) the question of how the
liberation takes place from the imprisonment in the ignorance of
the cave to the complete freedom conditioned by the knowledge
obtained outside the cave. The answer, as is well-known, is that
the liberation is obtained through an increased (dialectically
developed) understanding of the metaphysical concepts.   Or to
use a less historic example: What has determined the development
from pre-philosophic views of concepts like reality, truth,
existence, and validity to our days' philosophically advanced
criteria? Obviously, the answer cannot be that it is experience
since experience **presupposes** these concepts (is this or that
experience valid, true, real, etc.?). The answer is that the
development has taken place through a process of more and more
refined philosophical analyses of the concepts which are used in
order to describe the initial situation. To express it differently:
Through the philosophic analysis we obtain a deeper and greater
understanding of the concepts of which we already, before the
analysis began, had some understanding, although neither a deep
nor a correct understanding. They are concepts which constitute
the presupposition for all consciousness and consequently also for
all language.

In accordance with a more Hegelian language we may say
that the development - or movement as Hegel says - is determined
by the very nature of thought, (it is Hegelian to say the nature
of thought and not, for instance, the nature of thinking, just as

it is also Hegelian to speak about the concept; Hegel speaks about the concept of reality, the concept of validity, etc.; but he also speaks about the concept as such by which he means - which is not off-hand obvious - the conceptual system of philosophy). It is a movement, therefore, which is characterized, not by being contingent, but by being a necessary conceptual system. Due to its built-in logic a concept implies another concept. The concept of negativity, for instance, implies the concept of positivity. It implies this concept in the sense that the concept of negativity would not be understood unless the concept of positivity also is understood. To express it in a Hegelian language: The concept of negativity is understood by seeing what it is not. And what is true of the concept of negativity is true also of other concepts. The concept of freedom was examined when Schelling's philosophy was explained (cf. p.70 above). If it is not determined by seeing what it is not there is no determination of it at all. Any definition of it will be either too broad or too narrow - either it will exclude what ought not to be excluded, or it includes what ought not to be included. Only by seeing which particular kind of unfreedom that is negated is an understanding of the different uses of the word freedom obtained. To say about a person that he is free has meaning only if it is understood in which sense he does not lack freedom. The earlier given examples, which I shall not repeat here, clearly illustrate how the concept is understood by understanding what it is not.

. Every concept has thus an aspect of negativity built into its meaning - a negativity which is essential for a deeper understanding of the concept. According to Hegel philosophic thought and analysis is by necessity tied to the concept of negativity. Or expressed more Hegelian: The power behind the movement of thought is negativity. It is negativity which is the moving force behind the dialectical development or process.

Negativity is the very soul of the dialectical movement.[35]   A more
detailed examination of the dialectical process and method will
have to wait, however, until we get to its application to the
different problems of the **Phenomenology.**

Since there is identity between subject and substance,
between subject and object, the conceptual rules built into
consciousness and thinking (language) are identical with the rules
built into the object.   In other words, the dialectical process by
help of which thought arrives at knowledge is the very same as
the dialectical process governing the substance (the object, the
world or being).   It is a special Hegelian thought that the
Absolute, the universal subject or I, or what Hegel, using an
expression provoking to the modern ear, calls the World-Spirit,
through a dialectical development obtains absolute knowledge. And
since absolute knowledge is the knowledge and the path leading to
that knowledge, that the subject (the universal I) is identical
with the substance, the World-Spirit thus obtains self-
consciousness.   Despite the claim that the World-Spirit obtains
self-consciousness the World-Spirit must not be conceived as an
individual consciousness.   To express it paradoxically: The Self-
conscious World-Spirit has no consciousness of its own. It has no
consciousness over and above the infinitely many individual
instances of consciousness.   The World-Spirit does not belong to
a logical type of which it would make sense to predicate
consciousness.   The consciousness of the World-Spirit is displayed
in, and only in, the infinitely many individual instances of
consciousness.

During the history of mankind the World-Spirit has
progressed from one period to the next and through dialectical
steps toward self-consciousness.   Each period so to speak
inherited the knowledge accumulated by the preceeding periods.
It is a knowledge it has taken the World-Spirit - via the

individual instances of consciousness - millenia to accumulate, but each individual is able, however, through reading and instructions to learn the accumulated knowledge of the preceeding periods within a certain span of years.

The development of the World-Spirit (or the universal Ego) toward self-consciousness occurs by its own power. Nothing outside the World-Spirit (because nothing outside the World-Spirit exists) can determine the dialectical development. Thought, so to speak, is self-moving. That which is determined by the logic built into thought is, obviously, determined by (moved by) thought itself (thought and its built-in logic are identical). Each individual consciousness must, however, as just mentioned, acquire the knowledge already obtained through the preceding periods. Hegel speaks of inorganic and organic nature. An individual consciousness is, before its education has begun, confronted with that which the World-Spirit, or the universal subject, until then has been able to accumulate through its dialectical advance toward self-consciousness. The task for the individual consciousness is to acquire this inorganic nature. By being acquired by the individual consciousness the inorganic nature becomes the organic nature. The philosophical and cultural education of the individual consciousness consists, accordingly, in transforming the inorganic nature into organic nature. Expressed differently and in a more general way, philosophic and cultural education consists in the transformation of the individual and particular in the individual consciousness into the universal.

The three main stages or steps on the path leading to universality - the three stages of the dialectical movement, or as it may be expressed, the Hegelian dialectic writ large, are thus these: (1) The naive and uninformed consciousness which does not distinguish between itself and its object. Consciousness is

consciousness about objects but not consciousness about the
consciousness which is conscious about the objects. (2) At the
next stage consciousness and the objects of consciousness are
distinguished. Consciousness conceives of itself as a
consciousness confronted with a world of objects. At this stage
there is a radical difference between subject and substance. (3)
At the third stage the difference between consciousness and its
object, the difference between subject and substance, has been
overcome. By understanding that the objects of consciousness
necessarily have to be conceived by help of concepts and,
consequently, as determined by thought, the identity between
subject and object thereby follows. It is thus understood that
consciousness, by being conscious of an object which is identical
with itself, really is self-consciousness.

It would be natural to think that if the individual is
universalized it thereby loses its individuality. In a certain
sense this is correct, but in another sense it is not. It is
correct in the sense according to which individuality is conceived
in terms of the empirical and the non-rational. And since the
development toward the universalized individual precisely is a
development which eliminates the empirical and non-rational
elements, it follows that the individuality of the individual is
eliminated. But in another sense of individuality the individual
does not lose his individuality. He is now, the bearer of the
universal subject; he is now, and only now, the fully actualized
rational individual who therefore is the true and real individual.
He is what Hegel calls the concrete universal. A concrete
concept in distinction to the abstract concept is, according to
Hegel, a concept in which the particular exists not outside but
inside the universal, i.e. as an integral part of its meaning. In
this sense, and only in this sense, does the individual satisfy the

conditions for being a free individual. Because only then is he determined by his real Ego.

To the extent that individuals have universalized themselves to that extent they are identical. The individual differences are differences of an empirical nature and are differences which determine the individual as a particular individual. And these differences are precisely the differences which are disregarded when the individual is universalized. Individuals are different with respects to beliefs and opinions. To the universalized individual there is no room for beliefs and opinions. There is room only for the truth. There are no individual truths as there are individual beliefs and opinions. The individual who has acquired philosophical truth is a universalized individual. In a sense the **Phenomenology** can be regarded as a detailed and reasoned report of the path leading the individual toward his universalization. It is a path which is built into, or is a part of, the logical structure of reason and has of course nothing to do with the psychological structure of the individual mind. It is the aim of the following pages to describe this path. It is important to remember, however, that to Hegel, as it was to Fichte and Schelling, it is necessary to avoid Kant's concept of the thing in itself. This concept, which revealed a defect in Kantianism, was a great, probably the greatest, inspiration for the attempt to modify and to change Kant's conceptual model. But while Fichte and Schelling attempted to construct an alternative - the idealistic - conceptual model, Hegel attempts to discover the basic error which by apparent necessity led to the concept of the thing in itself. Much of what Hegel says in his **Introduction** (which follows the **Preface**) is devoted to such an attempt.

The Introduction

The basic error of Kantianism, and also, according to Hegel, of much of traditional epistemology, is, that knowledge is regarded, and is analyzed, as if it was a tool whose properties – i.e. its nature and limits – it is necessary to examine. Once the proper use and, accordingly, also the misuse, of the tool is discovered the temptation to attempt to use it on something which transcends its limits can be resisted. Kant's examination of pure reason was precisely such an examination. Pure reason was the tool – the instrument – through which knowledge was obtained. The Kantian model involves that there must be something (the stuff) to which categories (the tools) are applied. Since it is only **after** the categories have performed their work that knowledge is obtained, it follows that the stuff – that to which the categories are applied – exists **before** the application and, consequently, in itself is outside the limits of possible knowledge.

Hegel's criticism of Kant does not mean that he rejects Kant's philosophy in **toto**. If he did, it would contradict his conception of the history of philosophy as a dialectical development toward absolute truth. It would contradict his conception that each step, which in this connection would mean each philosophic system within the history of philosophy, is a necessary step, necessary, that is, as a presupposition for the next step. Hegel, consequently, acknowledges that his own philosophy, as well as the philosophic systems of Fichte and Schelling, to a great extent are conditioned by the Kantian philosophy. From Hegel's point of view, Kant's philosophy could be compared to the bud, Fichte's and Schelling's philosophy to the flower, and his own philosophy to the fruit.

Instead of what could be called the tool-theory, Hegel forwards the following theory. He begins by an examination of what counts as the lowest epistemological level. He begins with the state which, on a pre-philosophic level, must be accepted as knowledge. This is not just a psychological fact. Obviously, the logically necessary point to begin a philosophic investigation must be at the situation as it is, before there has been any philosophy at work. The beginning is to be compared to the conception of reality the prisoners have while enchained at the bottom of the Platonic cave. By the dialectical onward march the prisoners are liberated from the darkness of the cave until they finally, through the sunlight, see the truth.

The point of the Hegelian procedure is that it does not entail the concept of the thing in itself. According to this procedure knowledge becomes the result of the dialectical development. It is a development which involves that by each step forward that which ought to be negated is in fact negated. That which is not negated is preserved and becomes an element of (is **aufgehoben**) the next step. That which at each step was supposed to count as knowledge thus turns out not to be real knowledge. The advance toward knowledge takes place by destroying what necessarily must be destroyed. It is the force of negativity which conditions the advance.

In a sense consciousness is characterized by the nature of its object. To have consciousness of an object is to have a conception of the nature of that of which one is conscious - which is to say nothing more and nothing less than that to have consciousness of an object is to apply certain concepts, and it is the concepts applied which determine or constitute the nature of the object. To the extent that the conception of the object of consciousness is negated to that extent consciousness is also negated. In other words, there were no identity between the object as it is in itself (**an sich**) and as it is conceived to be (i.e. as it is **für** sich). The consciousness which is philosophically uninformed consciousness conceives the object of consciousness - the so-called external object - as an object which exists independently of consciousness. It constitutes something which is different from consciousness - it is what Hegel calls "the other" (**das Andere**). In a sense such a conception is correct. But in a certain other sense it is not. The starry sky exists independently of my consciousness. It would be absurd to deny that its existence is independent of whether I am conscious of it or not. But when the philosophically uninformed becomes less uninformed and understands what is meant by the universal subject he will be able to understand that the starry sky is not independent of the universal subject. He has then negated his previous conception and has consequently negated part of, and thus changed, his consciousness. It is essential to understand that it is not the object in itself (its **an sich**) which is negated; it is the conception of the nature of the object - that which the object is thought to be (its **für** sich) which is negated. It is also essential to understand that when the conception of the object is negated it is the conception of its nature, its metaphysical status, i.e. the applicable concepts, which is negated. It is not its existence as such which is negated. As the dialectical development advances the difference between the object **an sich** and the object **für sich** decreases. The aim of the dialectical process - the absolute truth - is reached when there is identity between the object **an sich** and the object **für sich**. The object in itself is then fully known. The Kantian demon of the thing in itself has been exorcised.

I shall now portray how Hegel conceives of the advance of consciousness from its pre-philosophic state - a state he characterizes as sense-certainty - toward absolute truth, i.e. from substance to object, from the particular to the universal, from individuality to universality.

Sense-Certainty

From an espistemological point of view the most primitive form of consciousness is the one which is constituted by the data presented by the sense-organs. It is the epistemologically most primitive form of consciousness inasmuch as it presupposes no theory, instruction or education. Every normal person possesses it. It is also the consciousness - and this is the essential point - which, **par excellence**, is conceived as presenting us with data which are particular of nature. Each datum can be named as an individual but cannot be characterized as universal. Later days' philosophic jargon uses the expression a 'sense-data language '. A sense-data language is usually regarded as a language which is epistemologically sterile.[36] From the fact that a sense-datum is red, or heavy, or round, nothing of epistemological interest follows. But precisely because it is a language which reports only what is immediately given it is also regarded as a language which constitutes the necessary basis for all knowledge.

An important difference exists, however, between the language Hume maintains as being the only language which can be epistemologically justified, and the language Hegel here examines. Hume's language was a sense-data language in the sense that whatever counted as experience (and only that which could be an object of experience had existence) was reducible to, and was in fact constituted by, sense-data. Some of the consequences of Hume's epistemology - consequences which he emphasized himself - were that words such as 'I','object' (object in the sense of being the bearer of, and therefore different from, the properties which are the properties of the object), and 'cause', all had to be eliminated from an epistemologically correct language (which, as we have seen, is impossible).[37] Whereas Hume's language was a language which, from a radical empiricist point of view, has eliminated words which constitute necessary conditions for having any language at all, the language Hegel examines is our ordinary language we all use and, consequently, the language which uses words such as 'I', 'here', 'this', and 'now'.   Contrary to Hume, Hegel does not examine the epistemological validity of such words; this is not his mission.   Instead his mission is to show that such words, contrary to e.g. Hume's view, do not name particulars but can be shown to stand for universals. To doubt the validity of these words would be to doubt the validity of the possibility of having any language at all. An alleged language which cannot identify the objects spoken about in space and time,[38] and cannot identify the person who speaks. The consciousness which Hegel here discusses, i.e. the consciousness of sense-certainty, is in other words a consciousness which by necessity must apply words such as a 'now', a 'this', and an 'I', - all words which seem to be paradigmatic of words designating particulars.

If it is correct that this language, which is assumed to constitute the basis for a description of reality, is a language neither possessing nor presupposing concepts, then, at best, it is problematic to assume the existence of such concepts. What Hegel attempts to show is that the assumption that the language supposed to be a description of or an immediate reference to the sense-given is in fact a language possessing concepts. He does not attempt to show (which would be an impossibility anyhow) that such a language is in itself incorrect. What he does attempt to show, is that it is our conception of it which is incorrect, (i.e. the conception that it is without concepts). Or to express it in a Hegelian way, our consciousness, at this stage, is false. As Wittgenstein asserted almost 150 years later, Hegel could also have asserted: Language is in order as it is.[39] Not language but our understanding of it may be erroneous. Or, which is the same, the **an sich** of language is not identical with its **für sich**.

Before Hegel's arguments are examined it should be noticed that Hegel does not speak about phenomena; he does not speak about that to which the words refer but about the words and their application; he speaks about their logical behavior. He does so for the simple reason that there is nothing else he can do. If by the word 'phenomena' one means such things as houses, trees, and spiders, it follows that there are no phenomena referred to by the words 'now' and 'here'. One may point to houses, trees and spiders but one cannot point to a 'now', a 'here', or a 'this'. Houses, trees and spiders belong to the furniture of the world. But among the furniture there is neither a now, a here, or a this.

Let me now turn to Hegel's arguments and let us begin with the word 'now'. To the concept of time the concept of a 'now' is fundamental. Together with the concept of 'before' and 'after' they exhaust, so to speak, what is meant by time. There is a difference, however, between these three concepts. Only the now constitutes what in a certain sense, is real. Past events no longer are. The headache I had yesterday I do not have today. Yesterday's headache no longer is; in a certain sense it is dead and therefore not real. Nor are future events real. The headache

I do not have but may get tomorrow may thus be a real event but
so far it is not.

The use of the words 'before', 'after', and 'now' depends on
the context.   We are **now** in the twentieth century, but
yesterday, which was a day in that century, is not 'now'. And
just as 'yesterday', 'today', and 'tomorrow' are systematically
ambiguous so are the words 'before', 'now', and 'after'. The word
'today' if used on Monday, refers to that very same Monday. But
if it is used the day after, it refers, not to a Monday, but to the
Tuesday on which the word 'today' is used. The use of the word
'now' behaves in the same manner. Tonight I can correctly say
"Now it is night."   Next morning I can, just as correctly, say
"Now it is morning."   The word 'now' is indispensable for a
language which refers to the sense-given world. At the same time
it does not itself refer to a certain once and forever given
moment.   There is a logical difference between the word 'now' and
such time determinations as 'the twentieth century,' or 'the 30th
of March 1985 at 11 o'clock a.m.'   Such time determinations are
uniquely referring.   They refer to respectively the twentieth
century and the 30th of March 1985 at 11 o'clock a.m., and
cannot be used to refer to any other periods or points of time.
The word 'now', on the other hand, can be used to refer to any
time whatever.

Hegel wants to emphasize not so much what the word 'now'
refers to as what it does not refer to.   According to its meaning
it is a selective word. And to be selective is to exclude
everything but one time determination. Whenever the word 'now' is
used it excludes an infinite number of time-determinations. There
are no limits to the number of past or future events, things, or
situations I could have talked about, but they are all excluded -
they are all, as Hegel says, negated - by the use of the word
'now'.   The function of the word - its logical behavior - is

accordingly determined by the dialectics of negativity. The word 'now' can be used to refer to any period, moment and time, or expressed in Hegelian manner, can be used to exclude any and all moments except one. It is due to these logical properties that Hegel thinks it justifiable to maintain that the word 'now' is a universal.

Hegel produces another argument by which he tries to show the impossibility of having any consciousness of a now. The argument is based on the metaphysical view of time as a continuous flow in which every moment is succeeded by another moment and where a moment has no time-extension, - if it had there would have to be a before as well as an after inside each moment and also an additional now at the very moment the before is going to be an after. The consequence of regarding time as a continuous flow is the paradoxical that the now disappears from time. The very moment one, so to say, points to the now, it has already passed away and belongs to the past. It no longer is; it belongs to that which has been. It has been succeeded by the next now - the now which the very moment it is born already belongs to the past. The now slides from not yet being in existence to already having been. It slides from one kind of non-existence to another kind of non-existence. At no time is it an existing part of time. The now that is right now - the now in which we have consciousness - is a now without extension; it is thus a now which either has not yet been or a now which already has been. The paradox is thus this. On the one hand the concept of the now is a necessary concept. It possesses exactly the same necessity as does the concept of time. On the other hand the now does not exist as a part of the content of any sense experience. It neither is nor can it be an object of consciousness. It is a misunderstanding of the logic of the now to conceive of it as a concept of something which could be an object of experience. Since the now does not have any extension and therefore is not a constituent of time, there is a certain sense according to which it does not exist.

What is the true meaning of the word 'now' is also true of the words 'this' and 'here'. The meaning of these words is not identical with that which they, so to speak, point to. That it is not, is easy to see. I can point to infinitely many things and can identify that to which I point by using words such as 'here' or 'there '. But these words cannot mean infinitely many things – if they did they could not, as in fact they can, be used in the both selective as well as the excluding way. As always with Hegel it is the negativity which constitutes the inner moving force of thought. A thing or a word is determined by that which it is not, by what it excludes. If I have five objects in front of me and I point to the fifth one, saying 'this' I have thereby excluded the remaining four. From a logical point of view this is correct, because if it was not the negative, i.e. the excluding aspect which was the decisive aspect, I had only specified at least the fifth but possibly also the other four objects.

Since a language referring to that which is sense-given by necessity must apply the words 'now', 'here', and 'this', and since, according to Hegel, they are universals, it follows that our prephilosophic view of such a language as referring to that which **par excellence** are particulars (i.e. which are located in space (the here and the this) and time (the now)) is wrong. Instead of being words which refer to particulars their use show that they are the negations of the particulars, i.e. they are universals. Since, furthermore, the words 'this' and 'here' can go proxy for whatever the sense-given might be, it follows that the language which refers to the sense-given cannot, contrary to our prephilosophic view, refer to particulars.

About those philosophers who view the external object as a real and, moreover, independent object different from all other objects and assume that such an existence is absolutely certain, Hegel (in a maybe not too elegant sentence) has this to say: "They **mean** 'this' bit of paper on which I am writing - or rather have written - 'this'; but what they mean is not what they say. If they wanted to **say** 'this' bit of paper which they mean, if they wanted to say it, then this is impossible, because the sensuous this that is meant **cannot be reached** by language, which belongs to consciousness, i.e. to that which is inherently universal."[40] Hegel's point is that language according to its concept can apply only words and expressions which are used as universals. Expressions such as 'external object', 'a real object', and 'a sense-given object' are all universals. If it should be objected that by the application of proper names one does say what one means - one so to speak points at the individual person by calling him by his name, - the Hegelian answer would be as follows. By using a proper name, e.g. A, it is always possible to ask the question: "Who is A?" (understood as the question of who is the bearer of the name). Obviously, the answer to this question cannot be by using another proper name. It must, in the last analysis have the form of a description (in Russell's sense), i.e. an expression which does not make use of a proper name.

Yet another objection against Hegel's arguments is the following. A concept has instances. The concept has what could be called a conceptual existence whereas an instance of the concept exists in a more robust sense. Hegel will have no difficulties, however, to show that the individual instance of the concept of man can be determined only through universals. It is more difficult to answer if the instances are sense-data. The content of a sense experience may be a white color. It is trivial about the instance of whiteness, i.e. the individual white color,

to say that it is white, but it would be absurd about whiteness to
say that it is white. A Hegelian answer would be that although it
is correct that the white color is white (to deny it would be to
violate the fundamental conditions for any use of a language); it
is nevertheless correct that the whiteness of the white color – the
whiteness which the individual white color possesses – is a
universal.

When Hegel asserts that the word 'I' is a universal his
arguments share the same logical structure as his arguments for
the universality of the words 'now', 'this' and 'here'. It seems
difficult to accept that a person who identifies himself by using
the word 'I' should not be an individual – should not possess
individuality. It seems difficult to accept that I who write these
lines should be a universal. However, as we have seen, it is
necessary to distinguish between the transcendental I and the
empirical I. The transcendental I is common property to all
language-using beings and is consequently a universal I. It is
more difficult, on the other hand, to maintain that the empirical I
is a universal. And yet. For the only way I can speak about
and identify my empirical I, and therefore think of it and
comprehend it, is through empirical data, which, as we have
seen, can be comprehended, described, and referred to only
through universals, and can be identified and have existence only
as universals.

Whichever way we look at it we are, concerning the language
of the sense-given and that which this language is about,
encapsulated in and captured by the universal. The particular
cannot even be an object for thought. Our consciousness, to the
extent it was structured by that which we thought and believed
concerning language and that which language was about, was
consequently a false consciousness. There was a gulf between

what it is in itself (its **an sich**) and that which we believed it was (its **für sich**).

The first step of the dialectical onward march has been taken; the first result of the power of the dialectical movement has been obtained. The new form of consciousness which presents itself after the negation of the consciousness of sense certainty is the consciousness of perception.[41]

Perception

The assumption that through language we should be able to name the alleged individual entities of the sense-given has been negated. Through philosophical analysis it has been shown that the cornerstones of such a language - the words 'now', 'here', 'this', and 'I' (what Russell calls egocentric particulars) - all are universal.

It has been maintained, at least since Kant, that sense-experience is possible only if that which is experienced is, or can be, classified as objects. Sense-experience thus involves an I who perceives and an object which is perceived. The I as well as the empirical properties of the object (what the logical empiricists called thing-predicates) are all encapsulated in language as universals. But an object is constituted not just by the empirical properties. It is also an entity, a thing; an object is conceived both as a class of empirical properties and as that entity of which the properties are properties. It is that which philosophers such as Locke and Descartes called the substance. Since the empirical properties constitute a plurality and that of which the properties are properties is a unity, it follows, that the concept of an object becomes something which is as well a plurality as a unity. It is

both one and many. As an object it is a **this** while that which
perception reveals is a combination of thing-predicates.

Among the properties which for instance a grain of salt
possesses are to be white, to be cubically shaped, and to have a
certain taste. A grain of salt, in other words, is partly a
combination of different properties and partly the substance (what
Hegel calls **die Dingheit**) which is the bearer of the properties.
The properties cannot be deduced from each other. It is not the
case that since it is white it follows that it is cubical; the
properties are combined in a conjunction; there is justification for
saying only that it is white and also (but surely not because) it
is cubical. What is justifiable, however, is to assert that since it
is salt then it is white and cubical; or expressed in a Hegelian
manner, since it is salt then it is the negation of all other colors
but white, and the negation of all other shapes but cubical. In a
way, therefore, it is determined by what it negates.

The object is thus threatened by a conceptual conflict. A
dialectical tension seems inevitable. On the one hand the object is
determined as this particular object, i.e. as an object which
exists in and for itself. On the other hand it is determined
through that which it negates, i.e. it is determined not by itself
but by other things.

Our conception of the object of perception - the object
perceived - thus possesses contradictory elements. It is in
opposition to itself and must consequently be regarded as
incorrect.

If instead of talking about perception and its object we talk
about language and its object it is possible to express the above
in the following way. Ordinary language is what could be called
(or in fact has been called) the thing-language.[42] We use this

language to talk about, not sense-data, but things or objects such as tables, stars, and spiders. Through this language we refer to, name, and identify things and objects. To perform this function the thing-language is inescapable. It is a language capable of making true statements. A philosophical system which implies that a sentence such as "There is a book on the table" cannot be used to make a true statement must by necessity be a mistaken system.[43] But as G.E.Moore emphasized in his famous essay "A Defence of Common Sense," there is a difference between understanding that which is said and to know the correct analysis of it. We all understand what is being said by the proposition: "There is a book on the table", but we are by no means certain of what the correct analysis is of, e.g., the concept of an object such as a book.

As already mentioned, the use of words such as 'this' and 'here' and, accordingly, the use of proper names, presupposes that whatever is pointed to by 'this' and 'here' and that which is referred to by the use of proper names already exist. And not only does it presuppose that it exists; it also presupposes that it exists as something, i.e. its existence is conceptually determined. An object to which no concepts apply, i.e. an object of which nothing can be said for the simple reason that no property can be attributed to it, is simply no object. An existence which does not exist as something is no existence at all. The only way an object can be determined is through its properties; it is through what Hegel called universals. It is this philosophical fact which led Berkeley and his phenomenalistic successors to maintain that an object is constituted by nothing but a combination of its perceived - actually or possibly perceived - properties or, rather, what Berkeley called ideas or perceptions, (in Hegel's above mentioned example it would mean that a grain of salt is constituted by nothing but, whiteness, cubical shape, and salty taste). There is

a difference, as earlier explained (cf. p.13f above), between the
question: "How is a certain object determined and identified - how
is its existence verified?" and the question: "What makes up,
what constitutes such an object?" The answer to the former
question is in terms of the, actually or possibly, perceived
properties; the answer to the latter question is in terms of, e.g.,
chemistry. But the answer to this latter question does not
provide an answer to the question - the question the
phenomenalists try to outflank: "Of what are the properties
properties?"

Another mistaken answer to this question is the one given
by Descartes and John Locke. Admittedly, this answer has the
appearance of necessity; nevertheless, it is metaphysically
unjustifiable to refer to a propertyless substance - an alleged
entity which is ontologically meaningless. To repeat what has been
emphasized above: An existence which does not exist as something
is not an existence at all; it is an ontological myth. Nor is the
Kantian answer justified. According to Kant the substance is not
an ontological entity but is conceived of as an instrument or a
tool, and an instrument or a tool requires to be applied to
something - which 'something' by necessity leads to the concept of
the thing in itself.

The aim of Hegel's analysis of the consciousness of
perception has been to show that our ordinary conception of the
objects of perception (tables, stars, and spiders) is false. It is
false consciousness in so far as the conception implies that the
object is an individual entity possessing its defining
characteristics (its essence) in itself. Philosophical (dialectical)
analysis, however, reveals that the object has its essence in
precisely that which the ordinary conception (the ordinary but
false consciousness) regards as the inessential, namely in its
negation, i.e. in that which it is not. A grain of salt is white

and cubical. As we saw, we may accordingly say that if it is salt it is white and cubical. A grain of salt is thus determined by its properties. But as we have also seen, it is, according to Hegel, in reality to say what it is not. It is in reality to exclude everything except the mentioned properties. To say that a grain of salt is white is to negate all other colors. Through dialectical thinking the consciousness of perception has been negated. The next step, the next consciousness of the dialectical consciousness is what may be called the consciousness of understanding.

It may be appropriate once more to emphasize that the **Phenomenology** is not a psychological description of the dialectical development of consciousness, but is a philosophical, i.e. a conceptual, analysis of the relation between subject and object - an analysis of consciousness and its object. As we have seen, Hegel explicitly distinguishes between what we think we (psychologically) mean and what through dialectical thinking we learn that we cannot mean; he distinguishes, that is, between our psychological state and the logic of our language.[44] It is curious to say the least that despite the fact that the **Phenomenology** is meant to be a description of the onward march toward the truth, a march where each step towards the goal is reached through dialectical thinking, it could be interpreted as a description of what in fact takes place. Even such a prominent philosopher as Nicolai Hartmann seems to hold such a view. In his well-known work **Die Philosophie des Deutschen Idealismus** he claims that Hegel deduces nothing (deduces even in the broad sense which includes dialectical thinking) and that he restricts himself to what is experienced.[45]

Another kind of erroneous interpretation can be found in Jürgen Habermas' **Erkenntnis und Interesse**. Habermas sees the **Phenomenology** as a history of emancipation. Werner Marx, in his earlier mentioned book (cf. footnote 14), says: "Jürgen

Habermas, in **Erkenntnis und Interesse,** has seen the goal of the entire movement of the **Phenomenology** in the recapitulation of the cultural history of the race as a history of emancipation. He has failed to notice that the goal of the **Phenomenology** can be concerned with nothing else but the unfolding of self-consciousness in its **truth.** This truth, according to the Preface, is nothing else but the whole of the scientific system. Self-consciousness knowing itself in its truth, i.e., as the system of its own determination, is absolute knowledge. It will not do to exclude the absolute knowledge from the **Phenomenology of Spirit,** and yet to employ the latter as a 'model' for a movement of emancipation."[46]

Understanding

In the consciousness of perception the conflict presented itself clearly. The object of perception was assumed to be as well an individual entity as a plurality. The consciousness of perception thus is a false consciousness. The next step in the dialectical movement toward the true consciousness and therefore also in negating the false consciousness is the consciousness of understanding. The **esse** of the object cannot be the directly perceived properties since it would entail that the object is what it is not - is what it negates. Nor can it be a Cartesian or a Lockean substance. The task must therefore be, as it also was for Kant, to find the **esse** not in that which is directly perceived but in something outside perception. The negation of the false consciousness of perception takes place **via** the consciousness of understanding. The **esse** of an object is not its **percipi.** Its **esse** must instead be found in **intelligi.**

Since, as already stated, to be is to be something; that is, to be is to be conceptualized. Whatever is can be comprehended only throught universals. The perceived object must accordingly be comprehended as a universal. And since, furthermore, the object of perception is independent of (unconditioned by) the directly perceived properties, it is what Hegel calls the unconditioned universal.

The task is thus to find an unconditioned universal which, by its very nature, is overcoming the conflicts - the contradictions - inherent in the consciousness of perception.

The concept able to do just that is the concept of force. Instead of a propertyless substance as e.g. Locke assumed, or instead of a category of substance as Kant taught, we thus get the concept of force. Force is the medium which unites the plurality. Force is the medium which creates the unity without which an object would not be an object. By help of the concept of force we are able to explain different phenomena; a force is able to explain because the essence of force is the law. An essential part of the meaning of the concept of force is the concept of **doing**. A force has to express itself; it does or effects something.

But according to Hegel, the concept of force is itself of a dialectical nature. It contains dialectical elements, i.e. each other contradicting elements. Hegel describes it this way: In order that a force can be actualized it is necessary that it is actualized by something which is able to solicit or incite it. A fire does not ignite everything; it lights wood and paper but not steel. Wood and paper are combustible; steel is not. Since the existence of a force is inseparably connected with its doings or with the ways it expresses itself, it follows that the existence of a force is inseparably connected also with the existence of something which is receptive to its solicitation. The difference between e.g. wood and steel Hegel would express by saying that whereas fire is solicited by wood into soliciting the force which solicits it, fire cannot be solicited by steel. Wood has the power to provoke fire (the force possessed by fire) to lighten it - a power steel does not have. From a modern scientific point of view, it may appear extremely unscientific; but however much the sciences advance, the principles remain the same: However complicated chemical equations the sciences are able to apply, sooner or later we get down to the basic fact that there are different molecular structures and that to be, e.g., inflamable is connected to a certain molecular structure.

A force which is not solicited or incited is passive; it is, Hegel says, a suppressed force. The force A may be solicited or incited to express itself as a force by B. B must thus possess the ability to solicit or incite the force A. In other words, B is itself a force. A and B are thus both forces and both depend on each other. A receives its existence through B and B receives its existence through A. Or to express it in a Hegelian way, the essence of A and B consists simply and solely in this, that each is solely through the other, and what each thus is, it immediately no longer is since it is the other.[47] But if a force can exist only through that which it is not – through its own negation – it follows that it cannot exist as a substance. A substance is precisely that which exists in and by itself and not through something else. A force exists only as a concept. Instead of a duplication of supposed forces we get the **concept** of a force.[48]

What we have seen so far is this: The contradiction inherent in the consciousness of perception was that the object was a unity as well as a plurality and that the essence of the object turned out to be that which was the unessential. In order to explain the unity of the object it was necessary to find an unconditioned universal, i.e., a universal which was unconditioned by perception. The unconditioned universal must be able to account not only for the unity of the object but also for its plurality. It was seen that the concept of force could not be a concept of an existing substance but had to be a concept of a thought (**eine Gedanke**). One may express this by saying that the ontological reality of a force is to exist as a concept while its existence as a substance is defined in terms of what is observed; that is, in what it solicits. In other words, force is determined operationalistically. The essence of force thus becomes its external expressions. By asserting the external expressions as being the essence of force, the concept of force has in fact been substituted by the concept of law. With the disappearance of the difference between force and its expressions force changes its essence. From being a concept of force it becomes a concept of law. It is the function of law to create unity out of a plurality, and by doing so it explains the plurality.

It is not difficult to see that the connection between a force and its observable expressions is of conceptual necessity. To illustrate this let us go back to the examples given earlier, (p.87). Consider such forces as ignition, push and pull. It is conceptually impossible to separate the force from its expressions. It is impossible to explain what is meant by an ignition, a push and a pull without doing it in terms of what happens when something is ignited, pushed or pulled. And it is impossible to explain what is meant by being ignited, being pushed and being pulled without giving a description of the special way these processes occur, i.e. of their regular or law-governed behavior.

The object - the object of the external world - is thus understood and explained in terms of the concept of law. Ultimately, then, the object is identical with the concept of law. Its essence belongs to the world beyond the senses (**die übersinnliche Welt**). As Hegel expresses it: "Within this **inner truth**, as the **absolute universal** which has been purged of the **antithesis** between the universal and the individual and has become the object of the **understanding** there now opens up above the **sensuous** world, which is the world of **appearance**, a **supersensible** world which henceforth is the true world, above the vanishing **present** world there opens up a permanent **beyond**."[49]

To identify an object of perception with the concept of law does not, at first, seem to be in accordance with our ordinary view. But by closer examination it seems to be not only a reasonable view; it even seems to be a necessary one. An object exists by necessity as a special kind of object. It is either a piece of wood, a tree, a stone, a horse, or something else. To exist is to exist as something. I know what a tree is, and I am able to identify it not just because it looks like a tree - so does an artificial tree or a make-believe tree, - but because it is as a tree should be. It behaves like a tree; or expressed differently, it behaves as it should behave according to certain laws holding for trees. However, to understand the growth and behavior of a tree involves an indefinite number of laws. A tree exists, and can only exist, in a certain environment; the environment is in interchange with the tree - it is affected and conditioned by such environmental elements as the soil in which it has its roots, the water, the air, and the sun. Indefinitely many processes, describable in terms of chemistry, physiology and in the language of other natural sciences, take place. In fact, there is no limit to the interconnection between the different scientific processes. The processes influencing the existence and growth of a tree are themselves explainable in terms of other processes, and so forth **ad infinitum**. If one had knowledge of all the laws (forces), one would also know that everything was dependent on everything. It is correct to say, therefore, that laws create unity where perception finds nothing but a plurality. The objective world is now brought under the concept of law. That is, the constant change, the coming into being and going out of being, the Heraclitian flux, which characterizes the world of appearances is now seen as determined by logos. But even so, there are still further steps to be taken before the dialectical process has reached the point on which Hegel says everything turns, namely "on grasping and expressing the true, not only as **Substance**, but equally as **Subject**."[50]

Although the external world (the substance) is comprehended under, absorbed by, and identified with the concept of law, it is still a substance which is conceived as an external and of the subject independent object. It is the Cartesian and Lockean substance, and the Kantian category of substance, which has been changed into the concept of law. But is is still an object which has to be, so to speak, metaphysically consumed by the subject before the consciousness of understanding has been changed into self-consciousness. This last but rather complicated phase of the dialectical process - **via negativa** - shall now be outlined.

The function of the laws of the different sciences is not only to describe how things happen but also, and primarily, to explain the occuring phenomena. Hegel's first step is the rather provoking one to challenge this very function. Without simplifying Hegel's arguments too much, it may be stated as follows.

A scientific law is conceived in a dialectical way: it is partly conceived as being descriptive and partly as being non-descriptive; it is partly conceived as having an empirical content and partly as being empirically empty. To the extent that it is descriptive, to that extent it cannot, of course, serve as an explanation. To explain is to be able to answer the question "Why?" and to describe is to answer the question "How?" If I ask why something is as it is or happens the way it does, I have not received an answer to my question if I am told that this is in fact the way it is. An answer to the question 'Why' must be in terms of a 'because', and a 'because' cannot be used in an answer which purely describes how things are. But even in a description some concepts are used which have an explanatory function. And concepts which are used in a description quite often can be understood only as concealing a law and consequently having an explanatory force. In other words, descriptions are seldom pure descriptions. A flash of lightening may be described by the ignorant person as a shining zigzag line. None of the concepts used in such a description have any explanatory value. But if it is described as a lightening, a concept of scientific (and explanatory) value is used. The concept of lightening is a scientific concept. What is observed is classified as an electrical phenomenon which involves other concepts such as positive and negative electricity. A phenomenon such as a lightening is then explained as an electrical discharge between the cathode and the annode. One is here dealing with non-empirical concepts. They are introduced because they serve an epistemological purpose. They do so because they make it possible to derive other concepts which enable us to predict different kinds of phenomena and thereby obtain confirmation of the applicability of the applied concepts. A phenomenon such as a lightening has thereby been explained; at least so it is generally assumed. But Hegel denies that this is the case. It is, he maintains, a misunderstanding to call it an explanation.

It is neither an empirical phenomenon nor an empirical fact that we have positive and negative electricity. On the contrary, they are concepts introduced to enable us to describe and understand certain aspects of the empirical world. The classification of electricity into positive and negative electricity is empirically empty. Not only do they cancel each other out; they also necessitate each other. The concept of positivity has meaning only as contrast or counterpart to the concept of negativity. One only knows the meaning of the word 'positive' if one also knows what it would mean if it were not positive, or in other words, if it were negative. This is why Hegel (who, as we have seen, prefers to express himself through the negative - he is the philosopher of negativity **par excellence**) expresses it by saying: "The positive is in its **own self** the difference from itself; and similarly with the negative."[51]

If one defines electricity (and accordingly determines its essence - which is what a definition does) in terms of positivity and negativity, it is a definition which only states a conceptual necessity. But is does not follow that it was a necessity to define electricity by using these concepts. The fact that it is epistemologically fruitful to do so is different from saying that is it necessary to do so. The classification of electricity in respectively positive and negative electricity is not enforced by something which is inherent in electricity itself. The classification is a product of consciousness; it is a product of the understanding. An explanation is, as already mentioned, an explanation only if it gives a satisfactory account of why something is as it is; i.e., if it is not just ascertained that it is as it is, but that it is what it is by necessity. But such a necessity cannot be based on the electricity itself (cannot be based on what Hegel calls the existence of electricity). The necessity, and therefore also the explanation, has its sole basis in the application of the concepts positivity and negativity. And since these concepts are the creation of the understanding, it follows that the explanation and the understanding of electricity are also the creation of the understanding. It is not only the explanation and the understanding of the electricity which are creations of the understanding; it is also the case with respect to its essence and existence, because electricity is **defined** by help of the concepts positivity and negativity. If these concepts are removed so is the concept of electricity itself.

Let me examine yet another example - an example Hegel himself examines. The law of motion has time and space as necessary elements. Without time and space it would of course be impossible to conceive of motion. Also necessary for a determination of the concept of motion are the concepts of distance and velocity. Motion is thus by necessity a relation between these elements and concepts. A difference between this example and the example concerning electricity should be noticed. Electricity as such, i.e. as a mere existing force, is different with respect to the concepts positivity and negativity. The definition of electricity in terms of these two concepts does not follow from an a priori given concept of electricity. The concepts of space, time, distance and velocity do follow, however, from an a priori given concept of motion. The concept of motion is by conceptual necessity connected with these concepts; they are part and parcel of the concept of motion. Electricity is defined in terms of positivity and negativity neither because it is a conceptual necessity nor because it is empirically given; it is so defined because it is epistemologically fruitful. Motion is defined in terms of a relation between time, space, distance, and velocity because it is a conceptual necessity.

There is yet another difference, however, between the two examples. When electricity is defined in terms of positivity and negativity, then two concepts are used which necessitate each other. Just as it is impossible to have, e.g., the concept 'bridegroom' without also having the concept 'bride,' it is impossible to have the concept 'positivity' without having the concept 'negativity'. So far as the concept of motion is concerned, it is otherwise. Not only are the concepts of space, time, distance, and velocity necessitated by the concept of motion, but these concepts have no necessary relation to each other. They do not necessitate each other. The concept of space does not entail the concept of time; and the concept of time does not entail space. To express it in a few words: So far as

electricity is concerned the applied concepts are not applied by
necessity; but their mutual relationship is a necessary
relationship. So far as motion is concerned the applied concepts
are applied by necessity, but their mutual relationship is not a
necessary relationship. Nevertheless, the laws of motion and the
definition of motion are expressions of the necessary mutual
relationship between these concepts. That the relationship is
conceived as necessary is itself a necessity. As emphasized many
times, the necessity is rooted in the very concept of an
explanation. An explanation (i.e. the answer to the question
'why') demands that the explicandum is conceived of as being
what it is by necessity. The question 'why' has not been
answered if the answer does nothing but to refer to how things
in fact are. The logical situation concerning the explanation of
motion is thus as follows. Through the definition of motion and
through the laws of motion the phenomena of motion have been
explained. The relationship between the concepts involved in the
laws of motion is a necessary relationship. This necessity is not
entailed by the logic of the involved concepts. It is therefore a
necessity which is rooted in consciousness. It is a product of the
understanding.

What all this means is, therefore, that what from an
ordinary, pre-philosophic view is regarded as an occurrence
independent of and different from consciousness in fact is a
"movement" of concepts. It is a maneuver of concepts of the
understanding.[52] The case of lightning, e.g., is understood,
explained and determined by help of two concepts which are
tautologically connected and tautologically cancel each other. The
concepts of positivity and negativity constitute two opposite
electric charges which through lightning are cancelled. We thus
have a relation of two opposites which negates itself. The purpose
of introducing two each other opposing concepts is precisely that

only then can they cancel each other. The cancellation or negation is not an outcome of external, empirical circumstances; it is a negation which is necessitated by the logic of the concepts. What is a tautology or a conceptual truth is of course not the existence of electricity; it is its explanation (i.e. the explanation of the different electrical phenomena). The explanation may be conceived as a dialectical conceptual movement. Its necessity belongs to the law of electricity and not to electricity itself. It is consequently only about the use of words.[53] It is a movement made possible through a distinction (the distinction between positivity and negativity), which is tautological and which consequently has the understanding as its source. It is because the distinction is a conceptual distinction which conceptually is cancelled that Hegel (who in his usual paradoxical way of speaking) asserts that it is a distinction which is no distinction. It is consequently also a necessity which is no necessity, and, consequently, an explanation which is no explanation. The above mentioned examples of laws, the laws of motions and the laws of electricity, are laws concerning special kinds of phenomena. Since there are indefinitely many kinds of phenomena, it is implied that there are, or could be, indefinitely many laws. But such a plurality of laws violates, according to Hegel, the principle of understanding. It is part of the structure of understanding that the plurality of laws should be reduced to a universal law. The goal or ideal is to find a single law which is able to incorporate all existing laws, and, accordingly, a law which explains everything. But the more general a law is, the less empirical content it has. A law purporting to say something about everything says in fact nothing. Hegel's example is Newton's law of universal gravitation. In both Kant's and Hegel's time, this law was seen as the most general law. A more generalized law was not known; a more generalized law was not even regarded as conceivable. What is gained by connecting the plurality of laws

into one law is that the universal unity required by the principle
of the understanding has been satisfied. But for this satisfaction
a price has been paid; it is empirically empty. It is a law, so
Hegel claims, in which the descriptive element has been reduced
to nothing. All it does, still according to Hegel, is merely to
assert that everything has a constant difference in relation to
other things.[54] However, to assert this is not an assertion
expressing a law; instead of being a law, it is the concept of a
law. But the concept of a law is not itself a law. What it does
express is that all reality is conformable to law - which Hegel
maintains is of great importance in so far as it is directed against
the thoughtless way in which everything is pictured as
contingent.[55] Obviously, if this is all the law says, it is the same
as a definition of what we mean by a law; and equally obvious, a
definition of what we mean by a law is not itself a law. A
definition of what we mean by a law cannot itself be one of the
laws falling under the definition. The conclusion Hegel arrives at
is that the law of universal gravitation is a law which neither
explains nor does it not explain, neither does it describe nor
does it not describe, because it is neither a law nor a
description.

There is yet another step of the dialectic movement to take
before we have finished the travel from understanding to self-
consciousness. But before describing that step, it will be useful
at this point to summarize the previous steps. In order to
overcome the contradiction inherent in the concept of an object of
perception (a contradiction not resolved by the consciousness of
perception) - the contradiction that the object apparently must be
both an individual entity and a plurality, - the concept of force
is introduced. Since a force requires another force in order to
solicit it, the result is a duplication into two forces. These two
forces presuppose each other. Each force is both the solicitor

and the object of solicitation; in Hegelian parlance: each force is what it is not, which means that force is not an existing entity, is not a substance. Force is accordingly a concept. And the concept of force turns out to be identical with the concept of law. To the extent that a law is not merely a description (in which case it is neither a law nor an explanation), it has both a descriptive and an explanatory element. But even the explanatory element, Hegel maintains, is no explanation at all.

The alleged explanations of electrical phenomena and of motion are used by Hegel to show that such explanations are nothing but tautologies, i.e., explanations which say nothing about the phenomena they pretend to explain. They are, however, true by necessity. But the truth is a triviality, it is a tautology, or, as Hegel says, only empty words. The change involved in the explanation is a conceptual change or movement, e.g. the change of movement from the concept of positivity to the concept of negativity.

It does not mean, of course, that changes do not occur. The world of phenomena is a Heraclitian world; it is a constantly changing world. What is rejected, however, is the alleged explanation of the changes. Hegel's analysis of the laws which allegedly explain the changes has as a result that the laws are based on the operations of understanding. The changes are consequently not changes in the object or the substance but, on the contrary, are anchored in the understanding or in, as Hegel also says, the I. In so far as this is accepted, it is also accepted that the object, the substance or the phenomena can be conceived, described and understood only as a result of the concepts of the understanding. Hegel has not yet concluded his arguments for how the understanding becomes self-consciousness. In his concluding steps, Hegel becomes dialectical to a high - and difficult - degree. In order to facilitate the understanding of

Hegel in this his last step let us keep in mind Hegel's example of
the positive and negative electricity.   What Hegel, in this
connection, is saying is this: An electrical phenomenon is
explained by the introduction of two tautologically connected
concepts between which a movement - a conceptual "movement" -
occurs.   It is accordingly to create differences which are not
differences and to create movements which are not movements.
This sounds like a paradigm of a formal contradiction, although,
of course, it is not.   It is, as mentioned before, Hegel's tendency
(perhaps desire) to express himself provokingly and in a
paradoxical manner. The meaning, however, is clear. There are
differences, because there is a difference between positivity and
negativity; but they are not differences, because electricity in
itself is indifferent with respect to positive and negative
electricity.   It is a movement, because it is a movement from the
positive to the negative pole.   It is not a movement, because it is
nothing but an operation of the understanding and not a
movement related to the objects.

As we have seen, Hegel begins his search for the
unconditioned universal by positing the concept of force as an
appropriate candidate for such a universal. As we have also seen,
there is no distinction between force and the expression of a
force, i.e. between force and the law. There is, for instance, no
difference between the concept of electricity conceived as a force
and the law of electricity, the law according to which electricity
is conceived through the concepts of a positive and a negative
pole. In addition to these two concepts - force and law - we have
all the infinitely many instances of the different laws. We have
not only the law of electricity and the law of falling bodies; we
have also infinitely many electrical occurrences and infinitely
many cases of falling bodies.   Such instances of the different
laws,   i.e.   occurrences   in   space   and   time,   constitute

appearances. Let us remember that what is being looked for is
not a justification for the existence of appearances; their
existence has never been doubted. What is looked for is an
explanation of them and therefore an understanding of them. As
we have seen, the concept of force - a concept which, as has
been stated repeatedly, cannot be distinguished from the concept
of law - is dialectical. A force requires to be expressed. It can
be expressed, however, only if it is itself incited. It must be
incited or solicited to incite or solicit. It is, as Hegel says,
"Force expressing itself and Force repressed into itself."[56] But
these distinctions are just as little real distinctions as are the
distinction of positive and negative electricity. To posit the
distinctions is at the same time to cancel them. Force or law is
thus a unity which has a duality built into it. Since the
explanation of the appearances has its ground in the law, it
implies that the duality built into the law is not only repeated in
the appearance (the explanandum) but is there expressed as
movement. Appearances constitute the arena of the play of forces.
It is a movement due to the conceptual fact that what is selfsame
repels itself from itself, and what is not itself selfsame is self-
attractive, or that like becomes unlike and unlike becomes like.
This conceptual fact constitutes, according to Hegel, a second
law.[57] By calling it a second law, Hegel contrasts it to the earlier
mentioned concept of law illustrated by Newton's law of universal
gravity. What this law, or rather conception of law, was
expressing was, according to Hegel, that everything has a
constant difference in relation to other things.[58]

Misleadingly, Hegel speaks about two supersensible worlds.
However, what he means is, not that there are two distinct
worlds, but that there are two laws applying to one and the same
world and that the laws are conceptual, i.e. they are non-
empirical; they are laws rooted in the understanding (the

intellect). The second law states that the selfsame repels itself
from itself and what is not selfsame posits itself as selfsame
whereas the other law states that the selfsame remains selfsame.
These two laws are plainly the opposite of each other. The
"world" in which like becomes unlike and unlike becomes like,
Hegel terms the inverted (**verkehrte**) world;[59] it is the inversion
of the other "world". Everything in the inverted world is the
opposite of what it is in the other world, i.e. of what the
inverted world is the inversion of.

Since according to the second law everything is the opposite
of itself, it follows that whatever is inverted is an inversion of
itself. In other words, it follows that the inverted world and the
world of which it is the inversion is one and the same world. But
if the one world contains the inverted world as well as the world
of which it is the inversion, nothing is excluded. Which is the
same as to say that the world is infinite.[60]

Appearances do not, therefore, constitute a world different
from the supersensible world (e.g., a Kantian thing in itself).
Appearances are part of the supersensible world, in fact it is its
essence, and the supersensible world appears as appearances.
When it is said that the supersensible world is an appearance, it
should be remembered that appearances to Hegel are not to be
identified with the sensuous world. Appearances, as was argued
in the chapter on Sense-Certainty, is the world of the 'this', the
'here', and the 'now' only in so far as these words are understood
as being of the inner and supersensible world. When it is often
said that the supersensible is different from the appearances,
then, so Hegel claims, it is because by appearances is meant the
sensuous and the perceived world as this world was conceived by
the uninformed consciousness. To the informed, i.e. the
philosophically educated consciousness, the sensuous and the
perceived world are both seen to be a supersensible world, or,

rather, to be one and the same, and the only, supersensible world.[61]

The one and only world includes the inversible world as well as the inversion of the inverted world. But since the concept of movement, based as it is on the supersensible law that like becomes unlike and unlike becomes like, is a concept of the understanding (the intellect), it follows that the world, the object of consciousness, or in classical metaphysical terms Substance or Being, is a movement of the understanding. The explanation of appearances, which implies an understanding of them, is thus to understand that consciousness understands that the object of its understanding is itself; "Consciousness is thus self-consciousness."[62]

When Hegel in his Preface writes (p.9f): "In my view which can be justified only by the exposition of the system itself, everything turns on grasping and expressing the True, not only as **Substance**, but equally as **Subject**" he has now, at long last and after deepgoing and exhausting although at times provoking philosophical arguments, arrived at what, at least to his own mind, constitutes the promised justification.[63]

If the world of Being, as an object of consciusness, is an inverted world as well as the inversion of the inverted world, i.e. is an infinite world, it is a world or a being whose essence is negativity. The power to negate is deeply engraved in Being. We are here reminded of Hegel's appraisal in the Preface of "the tremendous power of the negative" which is "the energy of thought of the pure 'I'."[64]

A reminder, often repeated, shall be repeated once more. The assertion that there is identity between subject and object is of course not an assertion about the individual subject. If I observe the flowers in the garden or the stars in the sky or human beings, I am most obviously not observing myself. As an individual consciousness I am satisfying the universal conditions for having consciousness at all. These general and universal conditions constitute the universal consciousness. But as it has been said before: The general or universal consciousness must not be conceived as an independent and special consciousness over and above the individual consciousness (or as an independent and individual subject or ego). The universal consciousness possesses consciousness only through the individual or empirical consciousness. The Hegelian assertion that consciousness by necessity is self-consciousness is consequently an assertion about the conditions of consciousness, the assertion, namely, that the necessary conditions for having consciousness also constitute the necessary conditions for the object of consciousness; that which conditions that a subject is a subject (an ego) also conditions the substance - conditions it in its essence as well as in its existence. Or expressed differently: The conditions for being a language are the same as the conditions for the existence of that which language is about.

Self-Consciousness

Lordship and Bondage

By dialectical thinking, Hegel has by now not just, as Fichte and Schelling, contented himself with the bare assertion of the identity between subject and object. He has (at least to his own satisfaction) also demonstrated it. By doing so he has demonstrated the thesis on which he in the **Preface** declared that everything depended. Step by step, or rather from consciousness to consciousness (from the consciousness of sense-certainty over the consciousness of perception to the consciousness of understanding), he has tried to prove that only self-consciousness is the true consciousness; only in self-consciousness is there identity between **an sich** and **für sich** - between in-itself and for-itself.

As earlier explained, there is a dialectical tension necessarily attached to the asserted identity between subject and object. It seems that what cannot be identified has been identified. A consciousness in order to be a consciousness must necessarily have an object. A knowing consciousness as well as that which the knowing consciousness knows is required. That which knows and that which is known must be just as different as, for instance, the finger which points at something must be different from that which is pointed at. The pointing finger cannot point at itself. But any finger can be pointed at by another finger. In a world where only pointing fingers existed (if there could be such

a world) there were nothing else a finger could point at but
pointing fingers. In general, one might say that fingers point at
themselves; or expressed differently: The pointing finger as such
(i.e. the "general" or "universal" finger) has as its object (i.e.
that which it points at) itself. But just as little as the universal
finger is a finger of flesh and blood capable of pointing, just as
little is the universal subject a subject possessing consciousness.
If consciousness nonetheless is attributed to the universal consciousness, it refers and can only refer to individual consciousness, since only individual subjects possess consciousness –
although an individual subject possesses consciousness only
because it satisfies the universal conditions for having consciousness, which is the same as to say that each individual consciousness is an expression of the universal subject. The universal
consciousness is that which remains when all the empirical and
individual elements have been subtracted from the individual
consciousness.

An essential concept in the Hegelian system is the concept of
becoming, (in Hegel's logic the concept of becoming is a
fundamental category). Just as, in the botanical system, the fruit
is presupposing the bud and the flower, so is the concept of
self-consciousness (i.e., the knowledge that there is identity
between subject and object) presupposing the consciousness of
sense-certainty, the consciousness of perception, and the
consciousness of understanding.

Yet another, and also often repeated reminder, should in
this connection be repeated once more. The description of the
development from consciousness to self-consciousness is not a
psychological or anthropological development; the description does
not consist of statements from any of the natural sciences. If it
did, it would lay open the **Phenomenology** to empirical
verification or falsification. The **Phenomenology** is describing a

logical, i.e. a dialectical development. The development of which the **Phenomenology** is a description is a story of how the concept of negation negates false consciousness and by necessity pushes it to its truth, (i.e., to consciousness which entails self-consciousness). Only a conceptual and logical development - not a psychological or anthropological development, - can have philosophical and metaphysical interest. The history of philosophy is the history of the development of the dialectical development of philosophic thought toward its truth. Such a description is different from the description, - and from a philosophic point of view irrelevant description - of the chronologically ordered story of the different philosophers' thought. Such a chronological story is philosophically relevant only if at the same time it expresses the dialectical development of philosophic thought.

To say that the dialectical development aims at truth is to say, among other things, that the aim of philosophic thought is the knowledge that there is identity between subject and object. Or expressed differently: The aim of consciousness is its truth - it aims at self-consciousness. In this connection Hegel uses the concepts of life and desire. The concept of desire is a psychological concept, and only by an extension beyond its ordinary use can it be used in such a way that its psychological denotation is lost. Hegel uses the term according to this extended sense. It is more in the sense in which we talk about the aim of thought as being the gaining of truth and about the aim of consciousness as being the understanding that it involves self-consciousness. Hegel's use is thus related to Aristotle's teleological concept of the potential aiming at its actualization. It would of course be misleading to say that the acorn desires to actualize itself as an oak; it is less misleading to say that the acorn aims at actualizing itself as an oak, and not misleading at

all to say that the growth of the acorn is directed toward the full
grown oak. Hegel's use is also, and perhaps more so, related to
the task set by Fichte's finite and limited ego to defeat the
opposition between the finite and limited non-ego.   But in
whatever sense the words 'desire', 'aim', and 'purpose' are taken,
there is only a short step from the movement determined by the
desire of consciousness to be satisfied - to arrive at its goal or,
expressed in Hegelian language, to become truth - to the
attribution of the concept of life to such a movement.

That consciousness desires to be self-consciousness involves
that consciousness (the subject) desires to incorporate the object.
From being an object independent of the subject - from being, as
Hegel expresses it, an other - it has to be identified with the
subject.   Only thus can self-consciousness be completed.   As an
'other', it represents the negative, and as a negative, it has to
be negated.   It has to be the subject in its otherness.

The struggle to incorporate the object as an other in self-
consciousness is mirrored in the section on **Lordship and
Bondage, (Herrschaft und Knechtschaft)**.   It is the struggle
to overcome the dialectical tension between consciousness as self-
consciousness which implies that the object for consciousness is
itself, and the object of consciousness regarded as something
different from consciousness regarded as an "other". This section
is by many Hegel-interpreters, if not surprisingly then at least
doubtfully, interpreted not as a philosophical essay but rather as
an anthropological and historical essay.   It is interpreted as an
explanation of how a society comes into existence rather than as a
further examination of the just mentioned problems connected with
self-consciousness.   In what follows I shall first describe the
socio-anthropological interpretation and next the alternative one.
The first interpretation is about the relation between the self-
consciousness of two individuals, whereas the second one is about

the relation between two aspects of one and the same consciousness. In describing the first interpretation I shall attempt to distinguish the conceptual aspect from the empirical-historical aspect. The difference is, among other things, that conceptual assertions are true by necessity whereas empirical assertions (i.e. assertions of a non-philosophic kind) are contingently true.

Consciousness becomes self-consciousness through a negation of the independence of its object. The object must be incorporated and be a part of consciousness. However, if the object of consciousness A is not object B but the consciousness B, it follows that B cannot be negated; it cannot be incorporated without losing its independence. At the same time, B's consciousness cannot become self-consciousness without negating A's independence. But if the dialectical development by necessity is aiming at self-consciousness, i.e. aiming at a negation of the object, it follows that if the object is another self-consciousness, there is a mutual desire to negate each other. No consciousness desires to have its freedom and independence negated; any consciousness desires that its independence and freedom shall be recognized or acknowledged (**anerkannt**) by anybody else.

Insofar as the genesis of self-consciousness is a conceptual development, it follows conceptually that a hindrance to that genesis will be resisted. A desire which does not resist or at least feel some animosity against any hindrance or obstacle for its satifaction has lost its right to be called a desire.

To this conceptually true assertion is added the contingent though reasonable assertion that in a fight between two individuals, one will be stronger than the other and consequently be victorious. Although the act of recognition is an act of freedom, the victorious person is able, at least to all appearances, to force the defeated person to recognize him. The defeated person is left with two possibilities: Either to be killed by the person who has defeated him, or to recognize him as a free and independent person. Since the defeated person out of these two possibilities prefers life to freedom (so goes the usual interpretation), he chooses to recognize the other person as the victor. Hegel emphasizes that only by being willing to risk one's life is freedom confirmed. A person who has not staked his life may be recognized as a person, but not as a self-consciousness.

The relation between the two persons is thus that the defeated person - the bondsman - recognizes the person who has defeated him - the lord. The lord, however, does not recognize the bondsman. As Hegel expresses it, the bondsman does not exist for himself but only for another; he exists only for the lord. The lord, however, does not exist for another but only for himself. This relation between lord and bondsman involves that the bondsman is forced to produce the material goods the lord wishes to consume. The lord enjoys (or in Hegelian language: negates) the goods but does not produce them, whereas the bondsman produces the goods, - not for his own enjoyment but exclusively for the lord's enjoyment. In other words, the lord is related to the goods - to the world of things - through the bondsman, whereas the bondsman is related to them directly. The bondsman is chained to the world of material things, whereas the lord has the power over it. The lord is able, although only through the work of the bondsman, to consume (to negate) it.

Since the bondsman is chained to the world of things, i.e. is chained to the world which is his working field, he is dependent in relation to it; he is dominated by it. And since the lord has the power over it, it follows that he also has the power over the bondsman. The lord has the power over - is independent in relation to - the world of things because he has staked his life in the fight for the recognition. By entering a life-and-death struggle, he has demonstrated his fearlessness of death and his independence of the world of things; he has demonstrated that he is unattached to the world the bondsman is fettered to. To be unwilling to risk one's life in order to win recognition as a free and independent person, proves that one is chained to the world of things and that a life without recognition is to be preferred to death. True recognition is enforced as a result of the life-and-death struggle.

The relation between lord and bondsman, conceived as a relation between two individuals, is subject to a dialectical process. A self-consciousness, in order to be a self-consciousness, must negate the independent existence of its object. If this cannot be achieved, which it cannot be if the object to be negated is another self-consciousness, a recognition is required. Only a recognized consciousness is able to be fully actualized as a self-consciousness. But the recognition the lord receives from the bondsman is precisely not a recognition from a fully actualized self-consciousness, because the bondsman is not recognized: he is not recognized by the lord. As Hegel expresses it, the outcome is a recognition that is one-sided and unequal.[65] The recognition the lord receives from the bondsman is from a self-consciousness which does not exist for itself but only for another. It is consequently not a recognition from which the lord can receive the true recognition of his self-consciousness. It is an invalidated recognition. The bondsman, who depends on the lord and has his reality, his being, not in himself but in the lord, is chained to the production of the goods which the lord enjoys. However, the relation between the lord and the bondsman changes radically due to the bondsman's dread (**Angst**). About this dread Hegel says: "For this consciousness has been fearful, not of this or that particular thing or just at odd moments, but its whole being has been seized with dread; it felt the fear of death, the sovereign lord. In that experience it has been quite unmanned, has trembled in every fibre of its being, and everything solid and stable has been shaken to its foundations."[66] It is this dread that is the beginning of the changed situation of the bondsman – the change from having an existence only for another to having an existence for himself; or, rather, to enable him to actualize the existence which he possesses potentially. But as just mentioned, it is only the beginning. The completion of the change, the completion of the dialectical process, is work. In contrast to the lord the bondsman has an immediate relation to the world of things and, accordingly, to work. To the bondsman the world of things is a world which exists independently of him. But due to his work on it – his reshaping of it – he, so to speak, finds himself in the results of his work. He projects himself into the work he has performed. The work becomes himself in his otherness.

The liberation of the bondsman from his bondage is thus mediated through dread and work. From dread for the lord, from the chains to the world of things, from an existence which is only for another, from an existence whose truth is in the lord and not in himself, it has become an existence whose truth is, not in the lord but in that which he has worked on, in that with which he is able to identify himself. It has become an existence which no longer is for another but is for itself.

The above interpretation is, as mentioned, an often accepted interpretation. It presupposes, as also mentioned, that Hegel speaks about a relation between two different self-consciousnesses, or, rather, two different persons. Before the alternative interpretation is described, it is of importance to examine the weaknesses of the just explained interpretation. It is not without interest to notice that many of the Hegel-interpreters who accept the "two-person interpretation" praise Hegel for the way he masters the dialectic which characterizes this chapter. Walter Kaufmann writes that next to the **Preface** the chapter on **Lord and Bondsman** is the most important. Findlay declares that Hegel when he, as Findlay expresses it, "suddingly swings over into the social sphere"[67] becomes much more lucid and illuminating. Kuno Fischer thinks that the section on **Lord and Bondsman** must be regarded as the most successful section in the **Phenomenology** and that it is a masterpiece of Hegelian dialectics.[68] And Alexandre Kojeve in his distinctly anthropological-political interpretation of the **Phenomenology** makes the relation between the lord and the bondsman a central point.[69]

A first point to notice is that if it had been Hegel's purpose to give an anthropological description of the genesis of societies then, in contrast to the **Phenomenology** as such, it would not be a chapter in philosophy but precisely in anthropology, history, and psychology. He would then expose himself to critique from the experts in these different scientific disciplines. Whatever one means by philosophy it is a trivial truth that philosophy is a discipline different from anthropology, from history, and from psychology. If a philosopher advances theories within such fields he obviously has stepped outside his expertise; he speaks as an amateur and not as a professional.

It seems, furthermore, that some of the statements Hegel makes he asserts without arguments. It is, of course, correct that if confronted with a choice between death and a life without freedom and the choice is life, then that is the same as to say that the one who so chooses prefers life to freedom and therefore is, in a certain sense, chained to life. But Hegel is not just saying this. He does not say that **if** one has to choose, then one's choice reveals one's preference. He advances the far from

trivial statement that a person who does not risk his life cannot
be recognized as an independent self-consciousness. Indeed,
according to Kojeve, it is a necessary condition for being a
human being. Only by risking one's life one becomes a human
being. Man thus creates himself as a human being.[70] But how is
the premise warranted - the premise that the relation between two
persons necessarily implies a life-and-death struggle, - a struggle
resulting in a relation between a lord and a bondsman? The
premise is neither a conceptual truth nor an empirically verifiable
proposition.

The concept of consciousness implies the concept of desire -
a desire to negate the independent existence of the object (the
object of consciousness), so Hegel maintains. The desire is a
desire for self-consciousness and this desire is satisfied through
the negation of the object. The difference between the desire to
obtain self-consciousness (i.e. the desire to actualize the
understanding that the object of consciousness is identical with
oneself, or, rather, is identical with oneself as universal
consciousness), and the desire to have another person to submit
to one's own will, is a logical difference. But the desire of
another consciousness to be actualized as a self-consciousness,
i.e. to obtain the understanding that its object is identical with
the universal consciousness of which it is a part, has nothing to
do, and is not in conflict with, my own desire for having my
self-consciousness actualized. That there are other
consciousnesses which also desire to become actualized as self-
consciousnesses can have no influence on the actualization of my
own consciousness as self-consciousness. It is, furthermore,
difficult to see what meaning, if any, it may have to maintain that
the understanding of a consciousness that its object is identical
with itself can be an object for my desire to negate it. It would
be absurd to maintain that every person desires to prevent that

other persons gain an understanding of themselves as self consciousness.

It also seems unwarranted to maintain that the life-and-death struggle is a condition for self consciousness. At least this is how Kojeve interprets Hegel. In Kojeve's words: "There is no human existence (conscious, speaking, free) without a struggle which implies a risk of life, that is, without death, without essential finiteness." Immortal man "- that is a 'square circle'."[71] It is unwarranted already for the reason that it involves a circle. A concept such as 'struggle for recognition' can be applied only under the presupposition of the concept of self-consciousness.[72]

In the light of these defects it is of interest to examine the possibilities for an alternative interpretation of Hegel's section on lordship and bondage.

The section occupies a central place in the chapter on self-consciousness. It seems reasonable, therefore, to believe that Hegel does not, as Findlay expresses it, "suddenly swing over into the social sphere," but is concerned about a further analysis and clarification of the metaphysical concept of self-consciousness - a concept which is of utmost importance to the Hegelian system.

Although it is correct, as Kaufmann asserts, that the expression "to be self-conscious" in German (as it also does in, e.g., Danish) means to be self-assured and proud,[73] but in this sense it is a psychological concept just as it is the psychological concept of self-consciousness which is involved if the interpretation is that Hegel describes the relation between two individuals who both desire and fight for recognition. But it would be wrong, not to say irresponsible, to change the meaning of the key concept, to change it from a metaphysical concept to a psychological concept.

In order to investigate the possibility of giving another and a more philosophic interpretation, it is necessary to examine some crucial statements in the **Phenomenology**. One such statement is the following: "Self-consciousness is faced by another self-consciousness: it has come **out of itself**. This has a twofold significance: first, it has lost itself, for it finds itself as an **other** being; secondly, in doing so it has **superceded** the other, for it does not see the other as an essential being, but in the other sees its own self."[74] Although the first sentence of this passage could be interpreted as if Hegel is talking about two different self-consciousnesses, i.e. about two different individuals, the remaining part of the passage makes it clear that this is not the case. The expression "it has **come out** of itself" (**es ist ausser sich gekommen**) as well as the expression "for it finds itself as an **other** being" (**es findet sich als ein anderes Wesen**) are expressions referring to, and can only refer to, one and the same self consciousness. This is emphasized when it is added: "for it does not see the other as an essential being, but in the other sees its own self," (**denn es sieht auch nicht das Andere als Wesen, sondern sich selbst im Andern**). This is in full agreement with the concept of self consciousness Hegel had arrived at in the last chapter. What the above quoted expression refers to is the dialectical movement from the supposition of the independence of the object of consciousness to the understanding that this supposition has to be negated; i.e., to the understanding that the object is identical with (the universal) consciousness. It must be emphasized that it is the universal consciousness Hegel talks about. Expressions such as "it finds itself as another being" and "it does not see the other as an essential being, but in the other sees its own self" have no meaning if the words "own self" are taken to refer to the empirical self, i.e. refer to that in space and time existing individual. Standing face to face with another human being I cannot meaningfully (except in a metaphorical sense) say that I am identical with him. If the words "own self " however, are taken in the metaphysical sense, i.e. in the sense in which the words are supposed to refer, not to the empirical self, but to the universal consciousness, it is no longer meaningless. We understand quite well (even though we may not quite know how to analyze) such statements as: "His understanding of the situation was identical to mine" or "With respect to mathematical abilities the father saw himself in the son." We also understand quite well statements asserting that two persons share one and the same self-consciousness; they share the universal self consciousness.

But even if there are convincing arguments for the interpretation that Hegel is referring to the dialectical movements between two aspects of the universal self consciousness, it is nevertheless a question whether it is possible, considering Hegel's use of the concepts of lordship and bondsman, to justify and to carry through such an interpretation.[75]

In this connection it is of fundamental importance to keep in mind the duality of self consciousness: pure self consciousness and object consciousness. This duality gives rise to, as mentioned several times, the dialectical tension between subject and object: At one and the same time they are different and identical. Although Hegel thinks he by now has proved that the object is identical with the subject it is nevertheless necessary, within one and the same consciousness, to distinguish between that which is thinking and that which is thought. The bifurcation of consciousness which constitutes the object was emphasized through Descartes' assertion that the I as a thinking substance was immune to epistemological doubt, - an immunity not warranted for the obejct of thought. It is important to notice that Hegel indeed maintains that we have to do with two aspects of one and

the same consciousness: "Both moments are essential, and their
reflection into a unity has not yet been achieved, they exist as
two opposed shapes of consciousness."[76] Hegel uses the term
'moments' which cannot meaningfully refer to individuals; the two
moments referred to are precisely the two mentioned aspects:
pure self consciousness and object consciousness.   Pure self
consciousness or the thinking and knowing consciousness, the
empirically empty consciousness whose logical structure is the
mere 'I am I'; and object consciousness, i.e.   that which
constitutes the object of consciousness - that which is thought
and known.   It seems unnecessary to emphasize that these two
aspects or shapes of consciousness in no literal sense can be
conceived as individuals.   When Hegel after the above quoted
passage adds: "One is the independent consciousness whose
essential nature is to be for itself, the other is the dependent
consciousness whose essential nature is simply to live or to be for
another.   The former is lord, the other bondsman," then the
words 'lord' and 'bondsman' must, obviously, be taken in a
metaphysical sense.   As Werner Becker says in **Selbstbewusstsein und Spekulation**: "It actually is a world-historical
masquerade in disguise."[77]

It should also be emphasized that the assertion about the
duality within consciousness is not a psychological assertion; it is
an assertion based on the logic of the concept of consciousness.
It is a necessary feature of the concept of consciousness that
both of the mentioned aspects or shapes exist. It is part of the
logical structure of such verbs as 'to think' and 'to know' that
there must be a subject as well as an object - that there must be
an I that thinks and an object that is thought, a pure self
consciousness and an object consciousness. It was emphasized, as
already mentioned, by Descartes. To Kant pure self consciousness
was the transcendental apperception, and the object consciousness

was constituted by appearances structured by the categories. By letting the non-I be posited by the I, Fichte is accentuating the dialectical tension between the two shapes of consciousness - a tension which, as we have seen, is also in Hegel's concept of self consciousness.

Against the assertion that the distinction between the two shapes of self consciousness is a necessary conceptual feature it may be objected that, e.g., neither Berkeley's nor Hume's philosophy had this distinction. And if this is the case it follows, so goes the objection, that it cannot be a necessary distinction. Philosophers of Berkeley's and Hume's stature, it is asserted, did not base their philosophy on a conceptual error! And yet. In **Three Dialogues** Hyles asks Philonous about his own existence. After all, he, Philonous, as a perceiving being does not perceive himself, i.e. his I. In his reply Philonous in fact limits the application of the **esse est percipi** principle to external objects and thus acknowledges tacitly an **esse est percipere** principle; which is the same as an acknowledgment of the conceptual distinction Berkeley's philosophy allegedly did not draw. And Hume accepts the problem but does not accept the distinction. Instead he declares himself a sceptic. The necessary existence of the problem and his admission that it cannot be solved within the framework of his philosophy ought to let him see that it meant a negation of his framework.

Pure self-consciousness and object-consciousness (lord and bondsman) are dialectically connected. Pure self consciousness is in its existence independent of the object. It exists for itself; it is related to the object via object consciousness. It is related through that aspect of consciousness in which the object is incorporated and negated. Object consciousness does not exist, therefore, for itself but only for another. It is instrumental for the negation of the object (the negation of its independent existence).

As mentioned in the chapter on Fichte the deeper reason for the infinite I to posit the finite I and the finite non-I was for the limited or finite I to be able to actualize itself as an ethical being. The ethical task for the finite or limited I was to actualize itself as the infinite and absolute I, in other words, the task was to negate the limited and finite I. This task was, as mentioned when Fichte's philosophy was examined, an infinite task and consequently a never completed task. If **per impossibili** the task should be completed it would imply the negation of the finite I. Hegel's concept of the desire of consciousness to actualize itself as self consciousness corresponds to Fichte's concept of actualizing one's self as an absolute being.

Hegel's concept of desire is of an infinite desire. It is a desire to negate (and incorporate) the objects. It is therefore an eternally unsatisfied desire. Object consciousness is involved in a process (a "work") which can never be completed. It, so to speak, provides pure self consciousness infinitely with negated objects. But precisely because object consciousness is engaged in a process which never can be completed it has to recognize or acknowledge the objects, which in this connection means that it realizes and accepts the situation. And since pure self consciousness, which is a consciousness at all only if it has objects, - the objects provided by object consciousness, - desires the actualization of itself as self consciousness, it follows that also the desires of pure self consciousness never will be satisfied.

In the essay "The Difference Between Fichte's and Schelling's System of Philosophy" from 1801, (i.e., six years before the publication of the **Phenomenology**), Hegel writes that the need for philosophy has its root in the contrasts in man's life.[78] The contrasts Hegel mentions are contrasts expressing the contrasts between a conscious subject and the object for that subject. It is, Hegel maintains, when his ability to unite what is in a conceptual conflict disappears that the need for philosophy is born.[79] The struggle to bring into harmony the two each other opposing aspects of consciousness ("the lord" and "the bondsman") is consequently of first rate philosophical importance. It is of first rate philosophical importance to overcome the dialectical tension which exists between the two aspects. The knowing and the known I; the knowing consciousness and the known content of the knowing consciousness. The life-and-death struggle is a struggle to unite these two aspects. The knowing I - pure self consciousness (I am I), - is in itself empty and is nothing without the content provided by the object consciousness. And the content is a content only if there is a consciousness whose content it is. They depend accordingly on each other and are forced to recognize each other. The goal is that the harmony should be provided through the object consciousness (the bondsman) which by philosophical thinking negates the supposed (i.e. on the pre-philosophic level) independent existence of the object and thus understands that it can, as content of consciousness, i.e. as substance, be conceived not only as substance but just as much as subject. For the consciousness of the bondsman the essential thing is the object consciousness. But to regard the objects as ontologically prior entails that consciousness is on an ontologically lower level. Since a consciousness, however, requires an object, a content, in order to be a consciousness, and since objects cannot constitute a content of consciousness if there is no consciousness, a mutual recognition is a necessity.

But what is the criterion for the correct choice between these interpretations? A criterion which compels one to choose

does perhaps not exist. Nevertheless, it does not seem difficult
to choose if one weighs the two possibilities. Either one chooses
to interpret Hegel as if instead of describing the necessary
dialectical structure of the concept of consciousness suddenly
begins to talk about subjects which do not belong to philosophy
but belong to anthropology and psychology. Either one chooses
to believe that Hegel is describing the background for the rise of
and the psychological conditions for having self consciousness,
and chooses to believe that Hegel treats these problems with more
poetic imagination, or to believe that Hegel, though in a
metaphorical language, describes the dialectical tension within self
consciousness - a tension which is a necessary feature of the
concept of self consciousness. That this latter interpretation is
the correct one seems also to be evident from the fact that when
Hegel deals with, what he terms, the unhappy consciousness he
presupposes this interpretation.

Let me try, as with Fichte and Schelling, to translate the
lord-bondsman relation into a relation between language and its
objects. Language is, as we have seen, conceptually dependent
on its object. In order to be recognized as a language it must be
about something. There seems therefore to be a conceptual
difference between a language and that which it is about, i.e. its
object. Or rather, it seems a conceptual necessity that language
is about a non-linguistic reality. But as have been emphasized
many times, this non-linguistic reality can be conceived only in
linguistic terms. In other words, the object of language turns
out to be of a linguistic nature. Language is incorporating its
object - its object is becoming part of itself. Or in more Hegelian
terms, language consumes or negates the non-linguistic object and
makes it identical with itself. It is one aspect of language: to
work on the non-linguistic world in order to transform it into

language. This aspect of language - the aspect connected with the work - is, in Hegelian terms, the bondsman aspect.

But a language requires a language user. Language is not part of the material world. Language is not discovered in the way, e.g., minerals are dicovered. Language is a product, not of itself, but of rational beings. It is obvious, therefore, that the language user - the I - cannot be part of language. In other words, the I is a linguistic and transcendental concept. The I is conceptually tied to language. Only language using beings use the term 'I' and only language using beings can be regarded as an 'I'. That is, an I, in order to be an I, requires a language, which in turn requires objects. But even though the I is not part of language it nevertheless can be talked about - the term I can be used in language. However, it can be talked about or used only in connection with objects of language, e.g., "He offended me" or "I am taking a walk." The bare "I am I" (the logical structure of self consciousness) is not referring to the objects of language; it is not part of language; it is not **saying** anything. Accordingly, the I as such needs the work of the bondsman or, which is the same, needs the aspect of language whose function (or work) it is to incorporate (consume or negate) the non-linguistic object into language. The I as such, i.e. the I when it is not related to language, is not even an I. It is this conceptual fact Hegel expresses by saying that the lord (the I) needs the work of the bondsman (needs a language which in turn needs objects of language). The I is not an I without a language and a language requires a language user, i.e. an I. Both of these aspects of

language are then conceptually tied together. None of them can
be nihilated. They therefore have to recognize each other.

The Unhappy Consciousness

Given the dialectical tension between the two aspects of self
consciousness, pure self consciousness and object consciousness,
the remaining problem is of course to overcome this tension. The
two aspects have to be united without nihilating any of them.
They have to be sublimated (aufgehoben) in a synthesis.[80] The
dialectical path leads from Stoicism over Scepticism and, as a
consequence, the unhappy consciousness. The final synthesis -
the overcoming of the dialectical tension, - is accomplished in
Reason.

Thinking is an operation with concepts and not with picture-
thoughts. And since concepts are not only constituting reality or
being (to repeat once more: to be is by conceptual necessity to
be something, i.e., to be conceptualized; what is not conceptualized is nothing and therefore has no being), but also are my
concepts it follows that thinking is movement within my self.[81]

According to Stoicism, so is Hegel's interpretation, self
consciousness finds freedom and independence by accepting
thinking as the object of consciousness.[82] By doing so, object
consciousness is severed from the objects of the external world.
Stoicism does not deny the existence of the external world; it is
not negated but ignored. It should be remembered that to
Hegelian philosophy the distinction between thought and being has
been sublimated (aufgehoben). But Hegel here describes
Stoicism. And to Stoicism, which is only at the beginning of the

dialectical philosophic development, there is a dualism between thinking and that which thinking is about.

Consciousness qua thinking consciousness is free. It is free because its thinking is determined by nothing but itself. But by this severance or isolation from the external world and by conceiving its essence in thought, a contrast between the universal and the individual is inevitable. The external world is - on the stoic level of philosophy - conceived of as constituted by individual objects whereas the object of thought is a universal, the concept. The flower as such is an individual object. The thought or concept of a flower (the concept, not the mental image) is, as just said, a concept.

Since Stoicism does not deny the existence of the external world the contrast is preserved, i.e. the contrast between thought and its object, between the concept and that which it is a concept of, between the universal and the individual, and between the unchangeable (the concept) and the changeable. The freedom and the independence obtained by Stoicism is therefore only an abstract freedom. It is, as Hegel says, not freedom but the concept of freedom. It is a freedom holding good for the world of thinking and the world of concepts, but it is not holding good for that which the concepts are concepts of.

Stoicism is a withdrawal from the outer world into the inner world. But by withdrawing from the outer or external world Stoicism withdraws - all according to Hegel - from that which in the last analysis constitutes the criterion of what is true and what is good. Thought, and therefore also language, requires an object, requires an other. Whether a thought, i.e. a proposition, is true or false, is determined by its correspondence or non-correspondence with the facts of the external world. But if the external world is ignored or disregarded then the criterion of the truth is likewise ignored or disregarded. It also becomes impossible to decide which kind of action would be the right one. Because by the right action one must necessarily understand the kind of action which leads to a better world, but if there is no criterion of truth there is no way of telling whether one state of affairs leads to a better world than another state of affairs. A thought or a proposition becomes therefore a thought or a proposition which is about nothing; it has therefore lost its right to be called a thought or a proposition.

If the concept of truth cannot be applied the result is Scepticism. Stoicism negates (i.e. negates the essentiality) of the external world and affirms that truth resides in the inner world. Scepticism, however, denies that it can have any meaning to speak about truth, be it in the outer or the inner world. And where the concept of truth is inapplicable there can be neither experience nor language, nor even thought. In other words, Scepticism implies not only epistemological chaos; it also implies ontological annihilation. The concept of Stoicism implies the concept of Scepticism, and the concept of Scepticism turns out to be self-destructive.

It is a fact, however, that even a sceptic must be able to speak, to have experiences, and be able to think. In other words, his behavior as a human being belies his philosophic theory. Scepticism thus implies a contradictory consciousness; it is a consciousness at war with itself. It is a consciousness which cannot be a consciousness because it denies the external changing world of individual objects as it at the same time recognizes this world as a condition of its existence. It is a consciousness which believes it has its freedom in thought, albeit thought lacking content and therefore is no thought at all. The sceptic must accordingly admit that it is a false consciousness. It is a consciousness which is conscious of the split and disunity of its consciousness. It is therefore an unhappy consciousness, (**das ungläckliche Bewusstheit**). It is an unhappy consciousness because consciousness desires its unity at the same time as it realizes the impossibility of overcoming this disunity. It realizes the impossibility of the task of uniting the unchangeable with the changeable, the inner with the outer, pure consciousness with object consciousness. Expressed in Hegel's metaphorical language it has to unite the consciousness of the lord with the consciousness of the bondsman. The unhappy consciousness regards as its essence the unchangeable and self-identical pure consciousness and regards the changeable object consciousness as unessential. But since it is conditioned by and has its existence through that which it regards as unessential it becomes itself unessential. It becomes that which, according to its conception, it is not. There is a contradiction between its essence and its being, between its **essentia** and its **existentia**. It is alienated from itself; as a consciousness it is condemned and accordingly a consciousness longing for redemption.

Hegel's description of the unhappy consciousness is often interpreted through historical and religious concepts. A pioneer work in this respect is Jean Wahl's **Le Malheur de la conscience dans la philosophie de Hegel** (1929); it was a work which inspired a new interest in Hegel in French philosophic and religious circles. Important arguments have, however, been advanced against such an interpretation. One such argument is that Hegel describes and analyses the dialectical concept of self consciousness and dialectical problems connected with it. And in so far as these problems are of a logical character they cannot be identified with a special epoch of world history. Somewhat simplified it may be said that different historical epochs can, per analogy, illustrate the different dialectical aspects of self consciousness. But whereas history, through its very concept,

is time consuming - as is the development of philosophic systems
- the dialectical (logical) aspect of self consciousness is no more
time consuming than is, e.g., the fact that certain theorems
follow from certain premises. What is time consuming, however,
is the process of deduction undertaken by the individual
consciousness. It is important, not least in Hegelian philosophy,
to distinguish between the psychological process of reaching an
understanding of the logical dialectical connection between the
different concepts (which of course is a philosophical activity in
which the individual philosophers are engaged), and the very
logical connections themselves, which it is the purpose of
philosophic thinking to grasp.

The unhappy consciousness is redeemed only through
reason. Through reason the absolute knowledge that there is
identity between consciousness and its object is actualized; the
knowledge actualized is that both are a display of one and the
same reason. This is the real and true meaning of the concept of
self consciousness: Whatever is, the individual consciousness as
well as nature, is a display of, conditioned and determined by
reason. The individual consciousness does no longer relate itself
to its object as to something essentially different from itself; on
the contrary, it recognizes itself in its object.

It will be remembered that Hegel in the Preface emphasized
that the truth neither is the result nor the dialectical process
leading to the result, but is the result understood as a result of
the dialectical process or development. It is necessary therefore
to understand reason as a result of the dialectical development
leading from sense certainty to the knowledge of reason of itself.
Only then is reason actualized.

Hegel's answer to the often mentioned dialectical tension
within self consciousness can be expressed as follows. Language,

in order to be a language, is about something. It has an object.
But with sufficient philosophic training (i.e. the understanding
of the arguments in the **Phenomenology**), it is seen that reason,
i.e. the logical categories of language and thought, constitutes
the necessary condition for whatever is. To understand, be it
nature, history or whatever, is to understand that the object or
phenomenon to be understood is an expression of reason, i.e. of
the logical categories. The study of logic is therefore, according
to Hegel, to study God's thoughts before creation: "Logic is
consequently to be understood as the System of Pure Reason, as
the Realm of Pure Thought. This realm is the Truth as it is,
without content in and for itself. One may therefore express it
thus: That this content shows forth God as he is in his eternal
essence before the creation of Nature and of a Finite Spirit."[83]

The **other** of self consciousness, which is both an other and
not an other, (both an identity and a non-identity), is thus an
other in so far as nature is different from consciousness but is
not an other in so far as it is determined by the same logical
categories. Both are an expression of reason (the identity of
identity and non-identity). As Hegel somewhere else says: "What
is rational is actual and what is actual is rational."[84]

Let me once more quote Herbert Marcuse: "The **Philosophy
of Mind**, and in fact the whole of the Hegelian system, is a
portrayal of the process whereby 'the individual becomes
universal' and whereby 'the construction of universality' takes
place." The dialectical ladder leading to the universality - to
absolute truth and knowledge - is long. Hegel is trying to show
- in fact thinks he has proven - the existence of reason in
nature as well as in mind. What Hegel calls **Geist** is the
knowledge reason has of itself. To describe and examine the way
to this knowledge would be to go beyond the purpose set for this
book. The purpose has not been to give a general description of

the philosphers treated, but to throw into relief what I regard as
an unavoidable metaphysical problem - even the deepest and most
fundamental problem within metaphysics.

Let me conclude this rather difficult chapter about Hegel's
Phenomenology by pointing out, what also Findlay in his book on
Hegel points out, that in Hegel's later works neither concepts nor
principles are dealt with, which have not already been dealt with,
even   been   dealt   with   more   thoroughgoingly,   in   the
Phenomenology. Anyone who has understood this work has
understood Hegel's philosophy (or to refer to Marcuse's above
quoted statement - which says only what Hegel himself says in
the Preface: Anyone who has understood the universalization of
the individual has understood Hegel's philosophy). And as Findlay
also says: "And a study of the **Phenomenology** has the further
advantage of being so extremely and uniquely difficult as to make
everything else in Hegel seem straight forward and plain-sailing
by contrast."[85]

It seems neither irrelevant nor uninteresting to quote what
the German philosopher Wilhelm Windelband said already in 1878:
"The generation capable of understanding Hegel's **Phenomenology**
is about to die out. Already now those who have read it from
beginning to end can be counted."[86]

Concluding Remarks

The object of the preceding pages has been to throw light on and to clarify a problem which human thinking in its dialectical development necessarily had to confront. It is a development which the history of philosophy is narrating. Philosophic thought from Kant to Hegel, the philosophy usually described as German or Absolute Idealism, is not an arbitrarily chosen chapter. It is the chapter in which the fundamental metaphysical problem has been most deeply perceived, most deeply investigated, and most deeply dealt with.

And not only was this problem - unavoidable for philosophic thought - perceived and investigated to the fullest, it was also - still within this short period ('short' measured by the entire history of thought as a standard), - logically covered. Other possibilities for a solution, if a solution is possible at all, than the solution here attempted seem not logically possible. It is, among other things, these facts which make it not just interesting but paramount to study the philosophers, or, rather, the philosophic problems here dealt with. They were philosophers who, in a period where the spirit and culture of Europe was at its pinnacle, represent the culmination of metaphysical thinking.

But however far philosophic thought may advance along the dialectical path - along the path of negativity - it remains a fact that the problem constituting the foundation of German or absolute idealism, the problem due to which German idealism came into existence, is independent of time and space, of history and geography. It depends solely on the logic inherent or immanent in our concepts. And since the use of the concepts whose inherent logic entails the problem is a necessity, it follows that the problem is logically inescapable. If it were not, i.e. if it had no conceptual necessity but had its roots in something of an empirical nature - if it for instance were rooted in something social, psychological or in one of the natural sciences - it would, from a philosophical point of view, be of no interest. This would be so, independently of however interesting it would be from such other points of view.

Still another thing makes the problem interesting. It is now a generally accepted view that thinking and language, consciousness, understood in the sense according to which it implies self-consciousness, and language and, consequently, also philosophy, are inseparable. There must accordingly be what could be called a language-criterion. It was, as we have seen, the language-criterion which revealed the untenability, or even break-down, of Hume's philosophy. His philosophy entailed a language lacking some of the words necessary for a language (words such as 'I' and 'object'). Nor did Kant's philosophy pass the language test: On the one hand Kant's philosophy entailed that concepts such as 'existence' and 'object' were categories and that space and time were a priori forms of intuitions. But on the other hand, his philosophy also entailed the necessary existence of something about which could be said neither that it was an object nor that it was in space and time. Kant's philosophy could not, therefore, be upheld either. Or rather, it could be upheld only if it could be corrected and modified in such a way that it did not fail the language-criterion.

It is interesting to observe the difference between the here applied criterion and the theory of meaning proposed and accepted by the logical positivists. As is well known, the logical positivists rejected any philosophic system and any philosophic proposition of which it could be proven that it was unable to be

verified (or falsified) through experience. Metaphysical systems
and propositions were all declared to be without meaning.
According to the language-criterion it is possible if not always to
verify them, then at least to falsify them. It is also interesting
to observe that precisely because Hume was a representative of
radical empiricism, the logical positivists were bound to accept his
system. We are thus confronted with the peculiarity that the
logical positivists through their restrictive theory of meaning
accept a philosophic system which according to the language-
criterion is rejected.

The movement from radical empiricism to absolute idealism is
an all-inclusive movement. With respect to the relation between
consciousness and the object of consciousness, between language
and that which language is about, all possibilities seem covered.
If this is so, then it must be the case that within this spectrum
of philosophic systems a conceptual framework can be found which
does not violate the language-criterion. It has been the aim of
this book not only to give, as clearly as possible, a presentation
of a fundamental philsophic problem, a problem which so to speak
lies at the root of metaphysical thought, but also to show that it
is possible, if perhaps not in all details, then at least in its main
features, to accept the conceptual frame of German or Absolute
Idealism.

The quintessence of Absolute Idealism may without falsifying,
though simplifying, be summarized as follows: Language is by
necessity about something different form itself (consciousness is
by necessity to be conscious of something different from itself).
This corresponds to the Kantian dilemma. It is a logical
impossibility, however, to give meaning to that which language is
about without conceiving it in terms of language. The concept
'that which language is about' is indeed a concept which is
fathered by - logically squeezed out of - the very concept of

language. To say that the object of language itself falls under
the concept of language corresponds to Fichte's conceptual frame:
That the non-Ego is posited by the Ego. Or rather, the absolute
Ego posits the finite or limited non-Ego as well as the finite and
limited Ego.

Schelling's philosophy of identity asserts that there is
identity between nature and spirit, "Nature is the visible spirit
and spirit is the invisible nature."[87] If the language-criterion is
applied to this philosophy, it implies that language and that which
language is about are identical; they are identical in the sense
that both are determined by the same conditions for all being and
therefore also for language. Language and that which language
is about are conditioned by one and the same absolute reason.
But since absolute reason, all according to Schelling, has neither
subject nor object and therefore can have neither subjects nor
predicates, it follows that it is unknowable. It transcends all
possible knowledge.

By conceiving absolute reason as the condition of what ever
is, Schelling seems to hold two different views. Sometimes he
speaks as if absolute reason is the condition in the sense of being
the ground, i.e. the cause; and sometimes he speaks as if
absolute reason is displaying itself in all being (somewhat as,
according to Behaviourism, mind displays itself in behaviour,[88] -
i.e., is identical with behaviour). When (fatally) he is holding
that absolute reason is the cause, it follows that it is
unknowable. But when he is holding that it displays itself in
behaviour, it is of course known.

Parallel differences exist with respect to the problem about
the condition of language. According to one sense of the concept
of the condition, it follows that such conditions cannot themselves
be part of language. They transcend language and cannot

therefore be spoken of. In another sense, however, they can. If it is asserted, as in fact Kant did, that concepts (and therefore also the categories) can have meaning only when used in judgments, it follows that they can be spoken of in a meta-language.

Schelling's philosophy, in so far as it entails an absolute transcending all knowledge, is unable to satisfy the language-criterion. It can do that as little as can Kant's philosophy with its unknowable concept of the thing in itself.

In Hegel's philosophy, Schelling's absolute has become the philosophical (dialectical) system itself through which it is seen that the unversal I and its object, the universal subject and substance, thought and being, in the last analysis are identical. Thus the absolute becomes precisely that which is known. Or expressed differently: The absolute is the dialectical process itself through which it is seen that also the object of language - that which language is about, - is submitted to the same categories. To say that there is identity between thought and being, is therefore the same as to say that there is identity between language and that which language is about. Let it be emphasized once more that Hegel's absolute is not only the insight that there is such an identity; it is such an insight together with an understanding of the arguments leading to it. Not just the end product of the dialectical process but also the understanding of the process leading to it constitute absolute knowledge.

It is of course not possible in a few sentences to summarize what this book has been about. Nevertheless, even if I may if not distort then at least simplify by doing so, I shall try to do it. The problem which dominates the development from Hume over Kant, Fichte, and Schelling to Hegel is an inescapable philosophic problem. It is a problem which lies, as said above, at the root of metaphysical thought. If what I have called the language-criterion is applied, it is impossible to accept either Hume's or Kant's philosophy; and the foundation of Schelling's philosophy, his absolute reason, must also be rejected. Fichte, Schelling, and Hegel all struggled with the problem, and to be quite satisfied with Fichte's and Schelling's systems is hardly possible. Nor with Hegel's system. But one great advantage of Hegel's philosophy over Fichte's and Schelling's philosophy is that Hegel's philosophy does not contain any non-cognitive element. It does neither rest, as does Schelling's philosophy, on an absolute in which, as Hegel expresses it, all cows are black, nor possess, as does Kantian philosophy, an unknowable thing in itself.

Short Biographies

David Hume

David Hume, Scot, sceptic and advocate of radical empiricism, was born in 1711 in Edinburgh and died, also in Edinburgh, 1776. No doubt with pride, but without snobbishness, Hume writes that he was of good (but not rich) family. His father was a descendant of the Earl of Home or Hume. His mother was a daughter of Sir David Falconer who was President of the Supreme Court of Edinburgh. When Hume writes about his "good" family, it is not, as I just claimed, out of snobbery; this it was not, first of all because he was not snobbish, and secondly, in those days such biographical data were appropriate to any biography. The fact that he was born and also died in Edinburgh does not mean that he had spent his whole life in Edinburgh. This he did not, he in fact travelled extensively. In particular he took delight in living in Paris. When the reception of his work **History of England Under the House of Tudor** disappointed him, he thought of emigrating to France. In his autobiography, he writes: "I was, however, I confess, discouraged; and had not the war been at that time breaking out between France and England, I had certainly retired to some provincial town of the former Kingdom, had changed my name, and never more returned to my native country."[89] Somewhere else in his autobiography, he writes: "There is, however, a real satisfaction in living at Paris, from the great number of sensible, knowing, and polite company with which that city abounds above all places in the universe. I thought once of settling there for life."[90]

Only 28 years of age, he published his major philosophic work, **A Treatise of Human Nature**. The thesis of Radical Empiricism with all its implications is here, if not always convincingly, then almost always elegantly, argued for. The book, however, was not well received; in fact, as he says himself: "it fell dead-born from the press." It must have been, or rather was a disappointment to an author who admits, as Hume does, that his ruling passion is to achieve literary fame. It was a passion, however, from which Hume later in life achieved deserved satisfaction. In his autobiography, written only a few months before his death, he writes that at last he sees many signs of his literary reputation, although he knows that he has only a few years to enjoy it. About his own character, Hume writes: "To conclude historically with my own character, I am, or rather was (for that is the style I must now use in speaking of myself, which emboldens me the more to speak my sentiments); I was, I say, a man of mild dispositions, of command of temper, of an open, social, and cheerful humour, capable of attachment, but little susceptible of enmity, and of great moderation in all my passions."[91] And again: "My company was not unacceptable to young and careless, as well as to the studious and literary; and as I took a particular pleasure in the company of modest women, I had no reason to be displeased with the reception I met with from them."[92]

In the history of Philosphy, two outstanding accounts exist of how great philosophers are able, in the face of imminent death, to meet their destiny with calm and philosophic dignity: Plato's description in **Phaedo** of Socrates' last days, and Hume's autobiography. There is, however, a decisive difference. Socrates, to his last hours, was engaged in a discussion with his friends about the immortality of the soul - an immortality Socrates was convinced he could prove. In contrast to Socrates, Hume, although officially a sceptic, was convinced that his death meant eternal annihilation. Not long before his death, the Scotch jurist, James Boswell, visited Hume. Boswell (a bit tactless one dares say) asked Hume, "if he persisted in disbelieving a future state even when he had death before his eyes."[93] Hume's answer was that the possibility for a future state was no greater than the possibility "that a piece of coal put upon the fire would not burn." Boswell also asked him if he thought of annihilation never gave him uneasiness, to which he answered that it gave him no more uneasiness than the thought that he had not been. In his autobiography, he describes his attitude to death thus: "I now reckon upon a speedy dissolution. I have suffered very little pain from my disorder; and what is more strange, have, notwithstanding the great decline of my person, never suffered a moment's abatement of my spirits; insomuch, that were I to name the period of my life, which I should most choose to pass over again, I might be tempted to point to this later period. I possess the same ardour as ever in study, and the same gaiety in company. I consider, besides, that a man of sixty-five, by dying, cuts off only a few years of infirmities; and though I see many symptoms of my literary reputation's breaking out at last with additional lustre, I knew that I could have but few years to enjoy it. It is difficult to be more detached from life than I am at present."[94] This was written August 18th, 1776. On August 25th he died.

Immanuel Kant

Kant, just as Hume, died in the city of his birth, namely Königsberg. But in contrast to Hume who had travelled extensively, and was received at European Courts and befriended with the aristocrats of his time, Kant spent his whole life in Königsberg. Kant was born in Königsberg 1724, lived and worked in Königsberg, died and was buried in Königsberg 1804.

Let us again compare with Hume. Hume published his epistemological main work when he was 28 years of age. Had Hume written nothing after that age, he would still have been world famous. His place in the history of philosophy had already been secured due to that work. Had Kant died before he was 57 years old, he name would have been unknown; because not before he had reached that age, did he publish his **Critique of Pure Reason**, the work which established him as one of the greatest philosophers ever. Admittedly, he had philosophized about its problems for the last twelve years before he wrote the book, but the actual writing of the manuscript, according to his own testimony, did not take more than four or five months from the day he began writing it. In a letter to Moses Mendelsohn, Kant writes: "For although the book is the product of nearly twelve years of reflection, I completed it hastily, in perhaps four or five months, with the greatest attentiveness to its content but less care about its style and ease of comprehension."[95] And, indeed, as every reader of **Critique of Pure Reason** will know, great efforts to facilitate the understanding cannot have been made by the author! The work, just like Hegel's **The Phenomenology of Spirit**, is a most difficult work to read.

When he was 16 years old, Kant was admitted to the University in Königsberg and he graduated six years later. In 1755, after having worked as a tutor at different private homes, Kant became a docent at the university. As a docent, he lectured more than 20 hours a week. In his first year, he lectured in logic, metaphysics, and mathematics; to these courses were later added a course in moral philosophy, theology and pedagogy - at times even geography. When in 1770 he became a professor, his teaching hours were reduced to 13 or 14 per week; and in 1789 - when Kant had reached the age of 65, - they were reduced to 9.

Kant remained, as did Hume, a bachelor all his life. According to rumors, he twice considered proposing, but he spent too much time making up his mind - each time the lady had finally chosen another man! Admittedly, the thought of Kant as a husband and family man seems a strange if not impossible thought. If he had been married, he would hardly have been able to live the almost pathologically rule-directed life, he in fact did live. Each morning at five o'clock, his day started by him having a cup of tea and a pipe of tobacco. While he was having tea, he was dressed in a robe and a nightcap (some sources report that on top of his nightcap he had his three-cornered hat in order to be protected from the light). Without changing his dress, he then prepared for his lectures, which usually were delivered in the morning (quite often the first one began at 7 o'clock). After his lectures he again dressed in his robe, nightcap, and slippers and worked until somewhere between noon and one o'clock. Quite often Kant was invited out for dinner, but if he were not, he would himself have guests for dinner. Later in the day he took his walk - a walk he never missed. Then followed work until bedtime, which was around ten o'clock. He preferred to walk by himself. The reason was not, at least not primarily, as one would expect from an intellectual of Kant's dimension, to be able to devote himself undisturbedly to philosophical problems; but rather, what seems to be less characteristic for a person whose life was devoted to the deepest philosophic problems, that a conversation during his walk would force him to breathe through his mouth; and this, he thought, was unhealthy. This feature seems to illustrate a duality which, somehow, characterized Kant: His body was slender and delicate, but his thoughts had enormous power; his external life was monotonous to the extreme, his philosophy, however, was revolutionary. In his everyday life, details that to others appeared to be inessential and insignificant, to him were of importance and tended to dominate his routine; but in philosphy, only what was great and essential had its place. His everyday life and daily routine characterized him as a pedestrian; in his philosophy, however, he attempted what few, if any, have attempted: to reveal both the greatness and the limits of reason.

Due to his delicate and weak health, Kant was immensely concerned about the way he lived. Since he thought (presumably rightly so) that a sedentary life was unhealthy and since his philosophic work forced him to such a life, he placed his handkerchief on a chair in a remote corner of the room; every time he had to use it (Kant took snuff), he had to walk over to that chair. It must be emphasized, however, that Kant's concern for his own health was not just the old bachelor's interest in himself, nor a mere interest in staying alive as long as possible. Kant believed that as a human being, he had a duty to preserve his health. Only by preserving one's health, could one administrate the talent which one might possess and in the best possible way perform the work, it was one's duty to perform. Kant did succeed in preserving his health relatively well until the

last few years of his life. He gave his last lecture in 1796. In
his earlier years Kant's lectures had been lively and inspiring, in
his later years they tended to be dry, uninspiring and even
boring; not to say (as young Fichte expressed it, after he had
attended one of Kant's lectures in 1798) soporific. A student from
his lectures in 1786-1787 reports that Kant's lectures to a high
degree lacked liveliness and that at times one got the impression
that he was about to go to sleep. Suddenly he would seem to
wake with a start and try to concentrate on the lecture.

In his later years, Kant was very weak. Almost blind, almost
without strength, physical as well as intellectual, without clarity
of mind, unable to recognize old friends, unable even to complete
simple sentences, - in this way Kant's life slowly faded away. On
February 12th, 1804, he died, and was buried on February 28th.
Almost all of Königsberg and many persons from all of Germany
attended his funeral. His coffin was placed in a so-called
professor vault. In the course of time, this place deteriorated
completely. By a thorough restoration, an attempt was made to
preserve Kant's grave for times to come. The restoration took
place at the centenary of the publication of the **Critique of Pure
Reason**, i.e. in 1881. It was possible to preserve the grave for
less than seventy years. For in 1950 Kant's sarcophagos was
broken open by unknown persons, and only the empty
sarcophagos was left.

Johann Gottlieb Fichte

It may remain a forever unanswered question whether Fichte
(1762-1814) had become the famous philosopher he became, but
for the fact that Baron (**Freiherr**) v. Miltig one Sunday was too
late for the sermon in the village church. When the Baron
expressed his regret for having missed the sermon, he was told
that a small boy who herded geese and was son of a poor
peasant, due to an eminent intelligence would be able to inform
him about the content of the sermon. The boy's name was Johann
Gottlieb Fichte.   When they got hold of the boy, he was indeed
able, almost verbatim, to repeat the sermon. The small Fichte
made such an impression on the Baron, that he promised to pay
all the expenses of his education. Whether Fichte had been able
to get a higher education without the help of the Baron, one can
only guess. It is not unlikely, however, that without it, the
world would not have had a Fichte as a founder of Absolute
Idealism.

In his university years and the years immediately after, it
was theology that was Fichte's main interest. But another
accidental fact secured Fichte for philosophy. The Baron, his
benefactor, died, and he had to earn his living as a private
tutor. And it was as a tutor, it happened: A student wished to
study Kantianism. Fichte who had neglected Kant's philosophy
therefore had to make a thorough study of it. Fichte became
enthusiastic about it and became an ardent Kantian. After having

quit a post as tutor to a Polish family, Fichte walked all the way from Warsaw to Königsberg in order to meet Kant. Although at this first meeting the still young and unknown philosopher was received by the world famous philosopher with little more than bare politeness, Fichte soon became Kant's protege. This was due, at least primarily, to a manuscript on the philosophy of religion Fichte had sent to Kant. It was a work which holds a thoroughly Kantian view. It expressed Kantianism to such a degree that when it was published, and published anonymously, philosophers around the world were convinced that Kant himself was the author - only published pseudonymously.

It is not without interest to notice that all the pioneers of German Idealism began as followers of their predecessor but they also, all of them, broke away from them. Fichte began as an admirer and follower of Kant's philosophy, but broke away from it. Kant publicly criticized and disassociated himself from Fichte and his philosophy. Schelling began as a Fichtean but was later critical of Fichte's philosophy and, to a certain degree of Fichte as a person.[96] And finally, Hegel was an admirer of the five years younger Schelling; but already in the **Preface** to the **Phenomenology**, Hegel dissociated himself from Schelling - and did it (without mentioning Schelling by name) in a not too gracious way.

When Fichte was 32 years old, he published his **Foundation of the Entire Science of Knowledge (Grundlagen der gesammten Wissenschaftslehre)**.[97] The fundamental ideas of this work he never abandoned or even changed; but by temper he was restless and active and was incapable passively to contemplate the course of history and the destiny of the nation. The Napoleonic War was raging and Napoleon's armies were a threat against Germany, a threat Fichte considered in all seriousness - much more serious than did e.g. Hegel. When the French troups

entered Jena, Hegel was more interested in saving his manuscript
of the **Phenomenology**, which he had finished only the night
before the battle at that city, than the saving of his country.
Often quoted is the following passage from a letter Hegel wrote to
his friend and benefactor, Niethammer: "The Emperor, that
world-soul, riding out to reconnoiter the city; it is truly a
wonderful sensation to see such an individual, concentrated here
as a single point, astride a single horse, yet reaching across the
world and ruling it."[98] Fichte's temperament and attitude did not
allow such a rather unengaged dissociation. There is a picture of
Fichte who with his not exactly slim figure and not exactly small
nose stands as a member of the Home Defense with drawn saber
and his leathern waistbelt packed with pistols. And while Hegel
finished his **Phenomenology** at the time Napoleon's army entered
Prussia, Fichte eagerly tried to get permission to accompany the
Prussian troops in order to inspirit them with his speeches. He
was informed by the King, however, that the all important thing
now would be acts and not speeches; speeches would be more
appropriate when the victory should be celebrated. When the
(hardly expected) victory became a defeat, there could be no
victory-speeches either. Instead Fichte delivered   during the
winter of 1807-1808 his famous **Addresses to the German Nation**
(Reden an die Deutsche Nation), - an exalted appeal to the
German people to develop and strengthen the nation, - stengthen
it not through external power but through education and
development of character.

To live a quiet and of external events undisturbed life as a
professor was not, what of course is not to be wondered, Fichte's
destiny. He obtained the Chair at Jena in 1794, but due to his
view that God could not be conceived as being different from the
infinite or absolute I, he had to resign already in 1799. In 1805
he was appointed professor at Erlangen but the Napoleonic War

forced him to leave Erlangen after having lectured there for only half a year. For a short while he lectured at the University at Königsberg. In 1810 he was appointed to the Chair of Philosophy at the newly founded University of Berlin and was the first academically elected **Rektor** (the preceding **Rektor** was appointed not by the professors but by the King), a post he held from 1811 to 1812.

Hume and Kant remained bachelors all their lives (as did several others of the known philosophers such as Plato, Descartes, who nevertheless was the proud father of a daughter, Malebranche, Spinoza, Leibniz, Locke, Wolff, Nietzsche, and others). But Fichte (as did Schelling and Hegel) lived in happy matrimony. His wife was a niece of the German poet Klopstock, worked at a field lazaret and contracted typhus. She infected her husband, but whereas she recovered from the disease, Fichte did not. On January 29th, 1814, he died.

Friedrich Wilhelm Joseph Schelling

While Fichte began as a shepherd and had to be discovered as the genius he in fact was by a rich benefactor, Shelling was born into an intellectual milieu. The year 1775 he was born in Würtemberg as son of a pastor who had the reputation of being a learned man. Schelling reached the same age as Kant (Kant died a few months before his 80th birthday,   Schelling 7 months after his 79th birthday).

As a child, Schelling was a wonderboy. Already at the age of 15, he entered Tübingen University - a university primarily for theologians. At Tübingen he befriended Hölderlin and, in particular, Hegel, both five years his senior.   Without being revolutionary in the ordinary sense, all three showed enthusiasm for the French Revolution, - an enthusiasm shared by several of the academic youth at the time. They were enthusiastic since they saw the revolution as a victory over the Bourbons and for freedom.   However, the enthusiasm was followed by a dissociation from the later phase of the revolution which, to them, was characterized by terror.

But when the revolution was in its beginning, and victoriously seemed to advance toward freedom, they embraced it with enthusiasm. The Marseillaise was sung and a "liberty tree" was planted in the vicinity of Tübingen. The university was under the domain of Duke Karl of Eugen, and when the news about the liberty tree reached him, he found it appropriate to reproach the young students of theology for their conduct - a conduct he thought was improper. An anecdote tells that when the Duke asked Schelling (who reputedly was the translator of the Marseillaise) if he did not regret what he had done, Schelling's answer was supposed to have been: "Your Grace, we all have our faults."

Already when Schelling was 17 years old, he had his first publication - an essay published in Latin about the fall of man. The year after he had another: **On Myths, Historical Fables, and Philosopheme of Ancient Times.**[99] Only 23 years old, he was called to the Chair of Philosophy in Jena. The years in Jena, i.e. from 1798 to 1803, were intellectually stimulating and prolific. It was a Jena whose milieu was marked and inspired by Goethe and Schiller from nearby Weimar. It was also Fichte's and the Schlegel brothers' Jena. At the home of August and Karoline Schlegel, artists and novelists met. The meeting between Schelling and Karoline Schlegel was decisive to Schelling. In 1803, after having obtained a divorce from Schlegel, Karoline was married to Schelling. The same year he gave up his professorship at Jena and took over a Chair at Würzburg. In 1806 he moved to Munich where he was selected a member and secretary of the Academy of Sciences. Later he became the president. The marriage between Schelling and Karoline Schlegel was a happy one, and when Karoline died in 1809, Schelling was grief-stricken and was for quite some time unable to concentrate on his work. In 1827 he moved to Munich in order to take over a professorship in philosophy.

After Hegel's death in 1831, his Chair was vacant for a long time, but in 1841 it was decided to call Schelling to Berlin, primarily to counteract what the Prussian authorities regarded as the negative influence of the all dominating Hegelianism. Already in 1846, however, he gave up lecturing and lived a semi-retired life. In 1854 he died.

Philosophically, Schelling was lonesome. At the beginning of his career, he considered himself a Fichtean. But his Philosophy of Nature was in conflict with Fichte's Idealism. Fichte accused him of being a materialist, and Schelling accused Fichte of being a subjectivist. The conflict between Fichte and Schelling is, at least to a certain degree, about words: Fichte's absolute is not the individual empirical I; it is the universal I; and when Schelling writes about nature, it is a nature which is the visible spirit (**Geist**); nature is in fact the spirited nature. According to Fichte, the individual consciousnesses as well as their objects are all determined by the universal I. According to Schelling, the spirit - reason - is the common element in nature and the individual consciousness. However, according to Schelling, but not according to Fichte, there is a development from nature to consciousness. Spirit in nature is on a lower level - what he calls potencies - than in the individual consciousness. However, the development Schelling writes about is not a Darwinistic development; it is a development in which one level - one potency - is regarded as a logical presupposition for the next one.

The conflict with Fichte was not only of a philosophical nature; it resulted in a personal break between them. The break between Schelling and Hegel, which was also of both a philosophical and a personal kind, was more painful. First of all, Hegel and Schelling had been close friends at Tübingen and the years immediately after. It was a friendship where the five years older Hegel was immensely impressed and influenced by Schelling. Nevertheless, as years went by, they developed in different directions. Schelling moved toward the romantic; Hegel moved away from it. When Hegel in his **Preface** characterized Schelling's Absolute (without mentioning Schelling by name, however) as a night where all cows are black, Schelling wrote to Hegel thanking him for the copy of the **Phenomenology** Hegel had sent him, but with a barely veiled regret about their disagreement. It was Schelling's last letter to Hegel, and Hegel never wrote to him again. Secondly, Schelling thought that Hegel, who after the publication of the **Phenomenology** was regarded as Germany's leading philosopher - a leadership which until then had been his - had plagiarised him. The earlier warm friendship had become a rather cool relationship. In fact Schelling felt embittered against Hegel. Heinrich Heine reports that Schelling to him had complained about Hegel. "Schelling, when I met him accidentally, speaks of Hegel who had "taken his ideas," and "it is my ideas that he has taken;" and again "my ideas" was the constant refrain of the poor man."[100] It is, however, correct that there is much in Hegel which can be traced back to Schelling. But the decisive difference ought not to be overlooked. An essential point shared by Schelling and Hegel (and Fichte has more than just the bare beginning) is the identity between subject and object. In Schelling's absolute, there are neither subjects nor objects; it is excluded from being an object of knowledge but only for artistic intuition. According to Hegel, "everything turns on grasping and expressing the True, not only as Substance, but equally as Subject." But Hegel's Absolute is not beyond possible knowledge. To the contrary: Knowledge, in the fullest sense of that word, is possible only when the Absolute is known. And here is the decisive difference: To Schelling the Absolute is separated from the world in the same way in which the foundation is different from that which it is a foundation of. This conception is to Hegel a type-fallacy. To Hegel the Absolute is the very dialectical process leading from sense certainty to self-consciousness, i.e. the consciousness which understands that it has itself as object. Absolute knowledge, knowledge of the Absolute, is accordingly knowledge of the philosophic system which shows the truth of self-consciousness. It is thus not the ground or cause of the dialectical process. It is this very process.

But Schellings's time was not yet over. When in 1831 Hegel died from cholera his chair remained vacant until 1841. The romantic Friedich Wilhelm IV, who had ascended the throne in 1840, called Schelling to Berlin in order to, as it was said, to weed out "the dragon seed of Hegelianism." When Schelling began his lectures the following was enormous. As Wiedman says: "There were not enough auditoriums to hold the massive audience, which consisted of both students and numerous representatives from all the educated strata, who wanted to hear the (almost divine) revelations from the famous philosopher's own lips."[101] Among his audience were Kierkegaard, Engels, and Bakunin - the founders of respectively existentialism, communism (together, of course, with Karl Marx), and anarchism. The lectures, however, became a disappointment. Kierkegaard's complaint was that Schelling was too old to lecture and that he himself was too old to attend lectures. Schelling's critique of Hegelianism is that although it explains the essence of things - i.e., it explains their 'whatness' (their **'Was-sein'**), - it does not explain their existence (their **'Dass-sein'**). It is the task of what he calls the negative philosophy to explain the **'Was-sein'** and the task of the positive philosophy to explain the **'Dass-sein'**. Hegel's philosophy cannot be deduced from negative philosophy. From the **'Was-sein'** the **'Dass-sein'** does not follow. This is of course the very problem of the ontological argument. According to Schelling, all the ontological argument can do is to argue that it is in accordance with the concept of God that existence must be attributed by necessity - if, that is, there is something **in re** corresponding to the concept. What validly can be said is therefore only that **if** God exists then he exists by necessity. If there is something to which the term God justifiably can refer then this 'something' exists by necessity. But we still need a proof that there is such a something. Whatever we know about the **'Was-sein'** of God it does not entitle us to deduce a **'Dass-sein'**.[102]

As a philosopher Schelling was lonely, - lonely in the sense in which neither Kant, nor Fichte, nor Hegel were lonely. There was, and there is, numerous Kantians - the young Fichte was one of them. Schelling began his philosophical career as a Fichtean. But even though Hegel in his youth was an admirer of Schelling then the **Phenomenology** signified a break with Schelling's philosophy. Kant's as well as Fichte's stars were still shining, although not as brilliantly as before Hegel became famous; but Schelling's star even if it did not disappear, at least faded after Hegel's star was rising.

Whatever one thinks of Schelling's philosophic system, - his latest works are often dismissed as mystical (a concept he himself tried to demystify), - it may be said that with him the human spirit reached one of its acmes. Such acmes are often reached where the poet and the philosopher are united in one person. They are reached where a harmony is created between the philosophizing poet and the poetic philosopher. Through Schelling's genius philosophic thought embraced the fundamental problem of consciousness and being while at the same time thought was poetically inspirited. Without this harmony and unification of poetic spirit and philosophic thought Schelling's position had been another and less known position. But with this harmony and unification he is one of the few who at a time in which the European intellectual climate and culture reached a great, if not its greatest, point, occupied a distinctive position as one of its creators and representatives.

Georg Wilhelm Friedrich Hegel

Hume belonged to nobility, Kant's father was a saddler, Fichte's a poor peasant, Schelling came from the intellectual home of a pastor, and Hegel's father was a civil servant in the revenue office and ended up with the title of **Expeditionsrat**.[103] Apparently, Nature selects her genii without regard to rank and class. But although Hegel was a genius, he was not, as was Fichte and Schelling, a child prodigy. Hegel was conscientious, interested and did very well in his school. He probably qualified as a model disciple. He began school when he was three years old. When he was five years of age he was admitted to the Latin School. At that time he already mastered, as his sister Christiane reports in a letter, "the first declension and the Latin words belonging to it."[104]

When he began his studies at Tübingen he was not the model student he was at the Latin School. He was by no means ignorant of the joys and pleasures associated with student-life, if not **Gesang**, then perhaps **Wein und Weib**, especially the former. To quote Wiedman: "Hegel was a well-liked participant at the frequent drinking bouts in Tübingen's cafes. Instead of preparing his theological coursework, he liked nothing better than to join the group of philosophizing wine sippers, take hearty doses of snuff, play Tarok, and make his audience laugh with his earthy, double entendre jokes. Often, he would return to the seminary quite late, and once the distraught dormitory senior supposedly called out to him: 'Oh Hegel, you'll drink away what little intelligence you have.' J.H. Faber, who became minister of Oberstenfeld, recalls the evening that Hegel came home in a far from edifying condition and had to be hidden by him from the Seminary police."[105]

He studied Plato, Kant, Jacobi, and several other philosophers, but his primary interest, almost a passion, was Rousseau and the French revolution. He rejected an invitation to join a Kantian club because, as he said, he was totally involved in studying Rousseau. Hegel's testimony when in 1793 he graduated was not too commending: "He did not neglect theological studies and worked zealously at sacred oratory but in his delivery he was seen to be no great orator. Not ignorant of philology, he devoted much labor to philosophy."

As Kant, Fichte, and Schelling, Hegel began his career as a private tutor; and as Fichte and Schelling, but not as Kant, he taught at various universities: Jena, Heidelberg, and Berlin. Although Hegel became the all dominating philosopher he was no success as a lecturer. One of his disciples, the later professor in aesthetics Heinrich Hotho, describes Hegel as a lecturer in no commendatory terms. While he was lecturing he was sitting, almost crouching, nervously turning the pages in his notebooks. His speech was continually interrupted by his throat-clearing and coughing. Each sentence was isolated from the other sentences, piecemeal and almost pell-mell and each sentence was uttered with strain. Nevertheless, to the interested, intellectually matured and bright listener and after having accustomed himself to Hegel's style and language his lectures were a philosophically inspiring experience. During his years in Berlin his fame rose enormously. He became the "Statephilosopher." An affair which illustrated his status in a not too flattering way is the so-called Bebeke-affair. A young philosopher (a privat-docent) at Berlin university,

Friedrich Bebeke, was deprived of his right to lecture (his **jus docendi**) after having published a very un-Hegelian book: **Grundlegung einer Physik in der Moral**, and after having made some derogatory statement about Hegel in his lectures. The dismissal was occasioned by a letter from Hegel (who was supported by two of his colleagues). Five years later (presumably due to Hegel's recommendation) he regained his right. The affair illustrates that what happens to many celebrities also happened to Hegel: they only very badly put up with criticism, - even Kant whose life was dominated by the moral law, got irritated at philosophers who questioned his philosophy. Karl Rosenkrantz, a Hegel-disciple who has written a well-known Hegel-biography, says this about Hegel: "As for those people who simply contradicted him, he was hard as nails, and he would need to be in an excellent mood to persuade himself to associate with them personally. He was capable of powerful anger and rage, and if he felt that hatred was in order, then he hated with a vengeance. He was equally terrible when rebuking someone. Any person he attacked would soon be all a tremble, and at times he would treat some unsuspecting soul like a schoolboy, giving him such a dressing-down that both the victim and the other people present would be shocked and alarmed."[106]

However, Hegel must have been easy to get along with. At his death Hegel's sister left a sheet of notes about her brother in which she says: "Took pleasure in Physics. Lacked all bodily agility. Must have been easy to get along with, for he always had many friends; loved to jump but was utterly awkward in dancing lessons. Tübingen: was a gay but not dissolute student, loved to dance, enjoyed the company of women, preferred one now and then but never raised hopes for the future for her; as an M.A. still wanted to study the law, was close to Schelling who was a few years younger. Pulpit delivery bad, not loud enough, faltering. Switzerland: more than three years, returned introverted, cheerful only in small and intimate gatherings."[107]

When Hegel was 41 years old he married the only 20 years old Marie von Tucher. At that time he had already a four years old son. When Hegel was in Jena he had an affair with his landlord's wife; the result was that she gave birth to her third illegitimate child. The child, the son Ludwig, after having stayed for some years with his mother and later with the widow of one of Hegel's friends, he finally, as a ten year old boy, joined the Hegel family. The relationship between father and son (and for that matter between step-mother and son) never was good; anyhow, the son complained that his step-mother did not treat him as well as she treated her own children and that he always lived in fear and without loving his parents. He enrolled in the Dutch colonial army but died in 1831, - the year after his father's death, - in Batavia from a feber disease.

Hegel was a very hard working philosopher. He was extremely well read and wrote many books. Nevertheless, he also found time for parties and card playing; in fact, the consummation of wine in Hegel's household was not small. During the social season several bottles of wine were bought every second day.

In Berlin Hegel had success. His fame remains not just a national fame; it became an international fame. His **Encyclopedia of the Philosophical Science in Outline**, (**Encyklopädie der philosophischen Wissenschaften**), the first edition of which was published in 1817, i.e., the last year he was in Heidelberg, was reprinted in 1827 and again in 1830. The **Encyclopedia** is an outline of Hegel's philosophy and has three main disciplines: (1) Science of Logic, (2) Philosophy of Nature, and (3) Philosophy of

Mind. In 1821 he published his **Philosophy of Law, (Grundlinien der Philosophie des Rechts)**.

Besides the above mentioned topics Hegel lectured on several other philosophical subjects. Most of his lectures have later been published, mostly on the basis of notes taken by students during his lectures. Among the subjects of such lectures are: The history of philosophy, the philosophy of history, the philosophy of religion and aesthetics.

When Hegel was at the hight of his career he caught cholera, and on November the 14th, 1831, after only 30 hours of sickness, he died. The following at the funeral was, as could be expected, enormous. Professors and students from all the faculties were present in the main hall (the Aula) of the university. After his own wish he was buried next to Fichte's grave.

Hegel's philosophy system had an influence on about all the different scholastic disciplines. And Hegelian scholars were given preference by the appointment at the different chairs. For some time no other philosophy than Hegelianism seemed possible. In a way it is understandable. Because if it is seen that the problem concerning the relation between consciousness and the object of consciousness, or between language and its object, is an inescapable problem, and if it, furthermore, is seen that the logical possibilities for a solution are exhausted through the philosophies of Hume, through Kant, Fichte, and Schelling, to Hegel, it follows that if Hegel's philosophy avoids the pitfalls, absurdities, contradictions, or weaknesses associated with the philosophies of the four other philosophers, then it is difficult not to be a Hegelian.

But precisely because the logical possibilities for a solution are exhausted, philosophy must, so far as this problem is concerned, come to a rest. It was as if human thinking had not only reached its peak; it was also as if it in reaching this metaphysical climax had no more powers left. Did Hegelianism signify the final end to all metaphysical systems? Nietzsche's provoking statement comes to mind that "the will to system represents a lack of integrity" and his further statement: "I am not narrow-minded enough for a system - not even my own system."[108] Obviously, the acceptance of such a statement depends, to a great extent, on what is meant by a philosophic or metaphysical system. But one thing is certain: Since the problem, or complex of problems, dealt with in the present book are, as emphasized many times, fundamental for the understanding of ourselves and the reality we try to know, it is not a problem or complex of problems one has to be narrow-minded in order to be occupied with. If one wants (prefers) to call Hegel's philosophy a system, which indeed one can, it can be summarized by saying that it maintains that the substance equally well can be regarded as subject.

It is not a statement Hegel just advances. It is a statement he takes great pains to demonstrate. He leads us, step by step, from one misconceived consciousness to another, - from sense-certainty over perception, understanding, to self-consciousness. And Hegel's concept of the Absolute is, in spite of the metaphysically sounding word, a very sober concept. It is the very dialectical process leading to absolute knowledge. It is not knowledge about anything empirically. It is not a knowledge, therefore, which enables one to predict. It is a knowledge about the dialectical logic ("God's consciousness before creation") and through which one understands the logical structure of reality and of the historical (the philosophical as well as the political) development.

The Hegelian philosophy, which may be characterized as the most fully worked out system of absolute idealism, inspired, also after its split-up into left- and right-Hegelianism, much of 19th and 20th Century philosophy: Existentialism, Marxism, Phenomenology, and in a kind of negative way, Logical Positivism. But none of these philosophical schools, with the exception of the last one, is a deepening, nor rejection of the metaphysical problem on which this book is based, the problem, namely, about consciousness and its object, or, if one prefers, about language and its object. The philosophic answer to this problem must be within the different conceptual possibilities constituting the spectrum stretching from Hume to Hegel. But since both Hume's and Kant's conceptual schemes led to absurdities and contradictions they had to be rejected. Left then, is only the conceptual scheme of Absolute Idealism. A philosopher who does not want to accept this is left with two possibilities. Either he has to show that Hume's or Kant's philosophy does not lead to the here described absurdities, or he has to give up the problem as, in principle, unsolvable - which is the same as to say that the fundamental metaphysical problem is forever impossible to solve. It is of little use to declare, as do the Logical Positivists, that the problem is a meaningless problem, and, consequently, only a pseudo-problem. Because the problem follows from the fact that we are beings endowed with consciousness and therefore beings having consciousness of something - follows, i.e. from the very fact that a language is a language about something. To declare that this problem is a meaningless problem is to eliminate the foundation for, among other things, the arguments for declaring something meaningful or meaningless.*

Notes

1. Cf. my article "A Note on the Logic of One of Descartes' Arguments," **International Philosophic Quarterly**, Vol.XV (1975).

2. That meaning presupposes personal identity and therefore cannot be its criterion, I have argued at some length in **International Logic Review**, (1970), p.107ff.

3. I have argued this point in greater detail in "The Metaphysics of the 'I'," **The Philosophical Quarterly**, Vol. 22 (1972).

4. It is interesting to observe that the early Wittgenstein had a concept of the role of language which was closer to Hume than to Kant. Language, according to the author of the **Tractatus** does not **create** the facts but **picture** them. That Kant had a more advanced view of the crucial role of language than had the Wittgenstein who wrote the **Tractatus** seems undeniable. As Stuart Hampshire says: "After the early experiments of Russell and Wittgenstein, most contemporary philosophers are probably convinced that the idea of 'the facts', which are already individuated in reality independently of our forms of reference to them, is an illusion that cannot be given a sense." (**Thought and Action**, London 1965, p.216). That there are basic similarities, however, on some essential points, between Kant's and Wittgenstein's philosophy, I have tried to show in "Wittgenstein and Kant", **Kant-Studien**, Vol.60 (1969).

5. For an attempt to solve this paradox, see J.N.Findlay "Time: A Treatment of some Puzzles ", **Logic and Language**, First Series, edited by A.G.N.Flew, Blackwell 1951.

6. **Critique of Pure Reason**, B.132. For an analysis of the crucial passage in the **Critique**, see my "B 132 Revisited" in **Proceedings of the Third International Kant Congress**, Reidel 1972. Reprinted in **Kant's Theory of Knowledge**, edited by Lewis White Beck, Reidel 1973.

7. **Critique of Pure Reason**, A.363-364.

8. Here quoted from **Kant, Philosophical Correspondance 1759-1799**, p.229, edited and translated by Arnulf Zweig, Chicago 1967.

9. A thoroughgoing examination of Salomon Maimon's philosophy is given by Samuel Atlas in his book **From Critical to Speculative Idealism. The Philosophy of Salomon Maimon**. Martinus Nijhoff 1964. In a letter to Reinhold (a long-time admirer of Kant, and follower of his philosophy who nevertheless in his later years became a follower of Fichte), Fichte writes (in 1795): "My esteem for Maimon's talent is boundless. I firmly believe and am ready to prove that through Maimon's work the whole Kantian philosophy, as it is understood by everyone including yourself, is completely overturned... All this he has accomplished without anyone's noticing it and while people even condescend to him. I think that future generations will mock our century bitterly." Here quoted from **Kant. Philosophical Correspondence 1759-1799, op.cit.**, p.28.

10. **Lectures on the History of Philosophy**, Vol.III, p.479, translated by E.S.Haldane, Routledge and Kegan Paul, The Humanities Press 1974.

11. In an open letter (August 7th, 1799), Kant writes: "I hereby declare that I regard Fichte's **Theory of Science** as a totally indefensible system. For the pure **Theory of Science** is nothing more or less than mere logic, and the principles of logic cannot lead to any material knowledge .... I am so opposed to metaphysics, as defined according to Fichtean principles, that I have advised him, in a letter, to turn his fine literary gifts to the problem of applying the **Critique of Pure Reason** rather than squander them in cultivating fruitless sophistries..." Quoted from Arnulf Zweig, p.253.

12. "What sort of philosophy one chooses depends, therefore, on what sort of man one is," **Science of Knowledge. First Introduction to the Science of Knowledge** 5, Edited and translated by Peter Heath and John Lachs, New York 1970, p.16.

13. **Ibid.**

14. In his book **Hegel's Phenomenology of Spirit**, Werner Marx says: "The conception of subject-object identity in German Idealism is founded upon Kant's idea of

"transcendental apperception," the idea that the pure subject - conceived as a structure of fundamental logical acts - employs its synthesizing power of conception to confer logical form upon the universe confronting it," p.XIX. The expression 'subject-object identity' has the same meaning as the expression 'the universal Ego'. In another place Werner Marx emphasizes this point: "But let us recall once more that, for Hegel, the self is nothing else but the transcendental apperception of Kant," ibid, p.49. Hegel's 'I' is related to Kant's transcendental apperception in the same way in which Fichte's and Schelling's universal and absolute Ego is related to it.

15. "The self's own position of itself is thus its own pure activity. The **self posits itself**, and by virtues of this mere self-assertion it exists." **Fundamental Principles of the Entire Science of Knowledge** I, p.96.

16. P.F.Strawson **Individuals**, London 1959, p.11.

17. I have argued this point in my article "Language and Its Objects," **Philosophy and Phenomenological Reserach**, Vol.38 (1977), p.239-246.

18. For a further analysis of the claim that language is a condition for being able to see, cf. my article "On Seeing" in **Danish Yearbook of Philosophy**, Vol.I (1964), or in my **Language and Philosophy**, The Hague 1972, Ch.IV.

19. "Investigations into the origin of language, like traditional theories about the beginnings of social and political organizations, have something of a quasi mythical character. They can pretend to be historical no more that ritual stories of what the gods did at the beginning of time. They may serve, as religious myths always have, as guides for attitudes and actions." **Problems in the Philosophy of Language**, edited by Thomas M. Olshenwsky, New York & London 1969, p.734.

20. For a discussion of whether the natural sciences are approaching the completion of their work, see Nicholas Rescher **Scientific Progress. A Philosophical Essay on the Economics of Research in Natural Sciences**, University of Pittsburgh Press 1978.

21. In one place Fichte expresses it thus: "If the account of this Act is to be viewed as standing at the forefront of a Science of Knowledge, it will have to be expressed somewhat as follows: **The self begins by an absolute**

positing of its own existence." And in a footnote to this
statement he says: "To put all this in other words, which I
have elsewhere employed: **The self** is a necessary identity
of subject and object: A subject-object; and is so
absolutely, without further mediation. This, I say, is what
it means." **Foundation of the Entire Science of
Knowledge** I, p.98.

22.   About the intellectual intuition Fichte says: "This intuiting
      of himself that is required of the philosopher in performing
      the act whereby the self arises for him, I refer to as
      intellectual intuition. It is the immediate consciousness
      that I act, and what I enact: it is that whereby I know
      something because I do it." **Second Introduction,** Heath
      and Lachs, p.33. See also **Nachgelassene Schriften
      1790-1800,** p.375. Schelling's view is close to Fichte's. In
      one place Schelling expresses it thus: "The source of self-
      consciousness is the will. Through the absolute will the
      spirit becomes directly aware of itself, or it has an
      intellectual intuition of itself," **Abhandlungen zur
      Erlauterung der Idealismus der Wissenschaftslehre,
      Schellings Werke,** edited by Manfred Schroter, 1927, I,
      p.325. The intellectual intuition as it is here described is
      close to, if not identical with, the concept of intention
      which is logically tied to the concept of an act. The concept
      of intention as it is used in connection with an act entails
      that the acting person possesses an immediate knowledge
      that he is acting and, at the same time, which act he is
      about to or has started to perform. To say that such a
      knowledge is immediate is the same as to say that it is
      neither based on observation nor is it inferred knowledge.
      This view of the concept of intention does not exhaust,
      however, Fichte's and Schelling's concept of intellectual
      intuition. They both assert that through the intellectual
      intuition direct acquaintance with the transcendental Ego as
      an acting Ego is obtained. But this is knowledge which in
      no way follows from the concept of intention and the
      concept of an act.

23.   In his two volumes work **Von Kant bis Hegel,** Richard
      Kroner says: "Schelling's system is in many respects clearer
      and simpler (although often more arbitrary) than the
      Wissenschaftslehre from 1794 [i.e. Fichte's work]; here
      and there it may even be regarded as a commentary to it."
      II, p.84.

24.   Cf. note 22, above.

25. About the artistic creativity, about the artistic creation and about the artist, Schelling has this to say: "Any creative ability is that through which art succeeds in fulfilling the impossible, the ability, namely, to eliminate an infinite contradiction in a finite creation." **Werke** II, p.626. Or: "What art creates is only and solely possible through the genius because the problem which the artistic creation has solved is to unite an infinite contradiction." **Werke** II, p.623. About the artist who has created his piece of art, Schelling says: "He is himself surprised and happy by this unification which he regards as a favour from a higher nature and which has made the impossible possible." **Werke** II, p.615. About this higher nature, he says: "This unknown, which brings the objective and conscious activity in unexpected harmony, is nothing but the Absolute." **Ibid.** And finally, about art, i.e. the creation created by the artist: "To the philosopher Art is therefore the supreme since it so to speak opens the portal to the Holy of Holiest where, as it were, burns in eternal and original unification in a flame that which in nature and history is distinct." **Werke** II, p.628.

26. When Schelling denies the reason is the cause of being, he is, of course, thinking of what Aristotle called the efficient cause. In Schelling's words: "The absolute identity is not the cause of the universe, it is the universe itself." **Werke** III, p.25. If the absolute identity (the absolute or absolute reason) is identical with the universe, then absolute reason is what in Aristotelian language is called the formal cause.

27. Cf. my "Knowledge of the Future," **Philosophical Studies**, Vol.X (1959).

28. In his book **An Introduction to Hegel**, G.R.G.Mure writes: "Hence to have introduced Hegel against a background consisting merely of his immediate predecessors and contemporaries would have given a most misleading impression of provincialism," (p.XI). It would not be to exaggerate too much to say that Mure's book is primarily a book about Aristotle, secondly about Kant and in between a little bit about Hegel.

29. A lucid but non-mathematical description of the revolutionizing view of the world seen through the eyes of an expert in quantum theory, can be found in **Other Worlds, Space, Superspace and the Quantum Universe** by Paul Davies, J.M. Dent & Sons, London 1980.

30. The first English translation was due to J.B. Baillie in 1910, (a second, revised and corrected edition appeared in 1931). Baillie translated the title as **The Phenomenology of Mind**, a translation which is generally agreed upon to be incorrect: The English word for **Geist** is not mind but spirit. In Walter Kaufmann's book **Hegel. Reinterpretation, Text and Commentary** (1965), the author has rendered a translation of the **Preface**. Finally, in 1977, a new translation by A.V.Miller (with a Foreword by J.N.Findlay) has been published. If nothing else is indicated, quotations are taken from Miller's translation.

31. "Wer die Vorrede zur Phänomenologie verstanden hat, hat Hegel verstanden," Herman Glockner **Hegel**, Zweiter Band, Stuttgart 1958, p.419.

32. **Phenomenology**, p.27.

33. **Phenomenology**, p.9f.

34. In his book **Reason and Revolution**, Herbert Marcuse writes: "**The Philosophy of Mind**, and in fact the whole of the Hegelian system, is a portrayal of the process whereby the construction of universality takes place'," p.90.

35. According to Hegel, it is due to what he terms the understanding **(der Verstand)**, that one is able to analyze a totality, - to find the elements which constitute the totality. This force or power of the understanding to perform such an analysis, Hegel identifies with negativity. About negativity Hegel has this to say: "The activity of dissolution is the power and work of the **understanding** the most astonishing and mightiest powers, or rather the absolute power... this is the tremendous power of the negative; it is the energy of thought, of the pure 'I'," **Phenomenology**, p.18f.

36. In my "The Language and Causality," I have tried to show the sterility of a sense-date language. **Dialogos**, (1977).

37. Cf. Chapter II on Hume, above.

38. This has convincingly been argued by P.F.Strawson. Cf. **Individuals, op.cit.**, Chapter 1.

39. "Every sentence in our language is in order as is," **Philosophical Investigations**, Oxford 1958, p.98.

40. **Phenomenology**, p.66.

41. Perception is the usual translation of the German **Wahrnehmung.**

42. Cf. Rudolf Carnap "Testability and Meaning," **Philosophy of Science,** Vol.3 (1936), p.466.

43. An excellent argumentation for such a view can be found in Norman Malcolm's "G.E.Moore: A Critical Exposition," **Mind,** (1960), p.92-98, (see especially p.97).

44. "It is a universal too that we **utter** what the sensuous [content] is. What we say is: "This, i.e. the universal This, or 'it is,' i.e. **Being in general.** Of course we do not **envisage** the universal This or Being in general, but we **utter** the universal; in other words, we do not strictly say what in this sense-certainty we **mean** to say. But language, as we see, is the more truthful; in it we ourselves directly refute what we **mean** to say, and since the universal is the true [content] of sense-certainty and language expresses this true [content] alone, it is just not possible for us even to say, or express in words, a sensuous being that we **mean.**" **Phenomenology,** p.60.

45. "He [Hegel] does not deduce at all; the result is not anticipated, self-consciousness not presupposed. He restricts himself to that which the subject 'experiences', to what is represented and to how the representation represents itself. In fact nothing is inferred neither from the subject nor from the object. He simply describes the experiences such as he step by step finds them." **Op.cit.,** p.381. However wrong Hartmann's above quoted view may be, it does not imply that Hegel's method is a deductive one. As Dieter Henrich says: "It can hardly be disputed that in no case can Hegel's theory have assumed the form in the strict sense, of a deductive theory," (**Hegel Jahrbuch,** 1974, p.248). The philosophical argument is not of a logical-deductive kind. Plato's arguments in his **Dialogues,** Aristotle's arguments (cf. his arguments that to learn is not to have learned, whereas to teach is to have taught), Descartes' **Cogito** argument, and Kant's transcendental logic cannot count as examples in a textbook of formal logic.

46. **Op.cit.,** p.40.

47. **Phenomenology,** p.86.

48. "Thus the truth of Force remains only the **thought** of it," **Ibid.,** p.86.

49. **Phenomenology**, p.87.

50. **Phenomenology**, p.10.

51. **Phenomenology**, p.93.

52. Jean Hyppolite explains Hegel's arguments for the lack of explanatory force of the laws thus: "Seeking the necessity of law, understanding creates a difference that is not a difference and, recognizing the identity of what it has just separated, ends up with simple tautologies which it calls necessity. This, one might say, is the soporific virtue of **opium**. Why do bodies fall according to the law? Because they undergo the action of force, weight, that is so constituted as to manifest itself in precisely this way. In other words, a body falls in this way because it falls in this way." **Genesis and Structure of Hegel's Phenomenology** of Spirit, translated by Samuel Cherniak and John Heckman, Northwestern University Press 1974, p.132.

53. "But in all these forms, necessity has shown itself to be only an empty word." **Phenomenology**, p.93.

54. **Phenomenology**, p.91.

55. **Phenomenology**, p.91f.

56. **Phenomenology**, p.95.

57. "And thus we have a second law whose content is the opposite of what was previously called law, viz. differences which remain constantly selfsame; for this new law expresses rather that like becomes **unlike** and **unlike** becomes **like**." **Phenomenology**, p.96.

58. **Phenomenology**, p.91f.

59. **Phenomenology**, p.96.

60. "Thus the supersensible world, which is the inverted world, has at ·the same time overarched (**übergegriffen**) the other world and has it within it; it is **for itself** the inverted world, i.e. the inversion of itself; it is itself and its opposite in one unity. Only thus is it difference as inner difference, or difference **in its own self**, or difference as an **infinity**." **Phenomenology**, p.99.

61. "It is often said that the supersensible world is **not** appearance; but what is here understood by appearance is not appearance, but rather the **sensuous** world as itself the really actual." **Phenomenology**, p.89.

62. **Phenomenology**, p.101.

63. About Hegel's arrival at the conclusion that consciousness is self-consciousness, Richard Kroner writes: "With this a concept of central significance not merely for the just stated section of the Phenomenology but for the whole of the Hegelian philosophy has been arrived at." **Von Kant bis Hegel II**, p.402.

64. **Phenomenology**, p.19.

65. **Phenomenology**, p.116.

66. **Phenomenology**, p.117. Strangely enough, A.V.Miller's translation of this passage omits the following sentence: "... denn es hat die Fürcht des Todes, des absoluten Herrn, empfunden." **Phänomenologie des Geistes**, p.148.

67. **Hegel. A Re-Examination**, p.95.

68. Kuno Fischer **Hegels Leben, Werke und Lehre**, Ersten Teil, p.327.

69. Alexander Kojeve **Introduction a la lecture de Hegel.**

70. "The scheme of historical development is thus the following: At the start the future lord and the future bondsman are both determined by a given, natural world which is independent of both of them: they are thus not yet true human, historical beings. Then, by risking his life the lord transcends the given nature, his given animal nature, and becomes a human being, a being who creates himself through his negative action," **op.cit.**, p.179.

71. **Op.cit.**, p.183n.

72. See, e.g., Stanley Rosen who says: "Interpreters like Kojeve, who assimilate Hegel's logic into the **Phenomenology** or provide us with an 'anthropological' account of Hegel, **drop the generic ego or universal spirit**. Thus Kojeve for example, is faced with the impossible task of generating finite self-consciousness from 'the struggle for recognition.'" **G.W.F.Hegel**, p.161. The **petitio principii** is also

emphasized by Werner Becker, cf. **Selbstbewusstsein und Spekulation**, p.112.

73. "Here it is relevant that the connotations of the term are in English and German. While being self-conscious often means being unsure of oneself and embarrassed, **selbstbewusstsein** means just the opposite: being self-assured and proud. Of course, the primary meaning in both languages is the same: self-awareness. But while this sense is most important, the other connotations are relevant." **Hegel. Reinterpretation, Texts and Commentary, op.cit.**, p.152f.

74. **Phenomenology**, p.111.

75. Against a two-person interpretation and for one of a two-aspects of one and the same consciousness, argues Werner Becker in his books **Idealistische und materialistische Dialektik, Das Verhältnis von Herrschaft und Knechtschaft bei Hegel und Marx. Hegel's Phänomenologie des Geistes** and **Selbstbewusstsein und Spekulation.** And Eugen Fink in his book **Hegel** writes that Hegel by his metaphorical use of the figures of lord and bondsman is in danger of being misunderstood; he is in danger of being taken to engage in social philosophical problems instead of the ontological problem of the self-consciousness. It is interesting to observe that Findlay, who in his earlier mentioned book on Hegel (of 1958) interpreted the section on lord and bondsman as an essay on social philosophy, now (in his commentary to A.V.Miller's translation of the **Phenomenology**, published 1977) writes: "That the two self-consciousnesses are at bottom the same becomes deeply veiled," **op.cit.**, p.521.

76. **Phenomenology**, p.115.

77. **Phenomenology**, p.118.

78. Translated from the German by H.S. Harris and Walter Cerf, State University of New York Press 1977.

79. "When the might of the union vanishes from the life of men and the antitheses lose their living connection and reciprocity and gain independence, the need of philosophy arise," **op.cit.**, p.91. In his book **Vernuft und Welt** (p.2), Werner Marx says that this Hegelian pronouncement expresses the presupposition as well as the aim of German Idealism.

80. Hegel's use of the verb **zu aufheben**, at least more often than not, implies a combination of negation and preservation, **(aufbewahren)**.

81. "The Notion is for me straightway **my** Notion. In thinking **I am free**, because I am not in an other, but remain simply and solely in communion with myself, and the object, which is for me the **essential** being, is in undivided unity my being-for-myself, and my activity in conceptual thinking is a movement within myself," **Phenomenology**, p.120.

82. In his book **Hegels Phanomenologie des Geistes**, Werner Becker challenges Hegel's interpretation of Stoicism. **Op.cit.**, p.71ff.

83. **Science of Logic**, translated by W.H.Johnston and L.G.Struthers, Vol.I, p.60.

84. **The Philosophy of Right**, "Preface," p.9. Translated and edited by T.H. Knox.

85. **Op.cit.**, p.148.

86. Quoted from **Hegel Studien, Beiheft** 3 (1964), p.62f.

87. **Werke** I, p.706. Walter Kasper, in his book **Das Absolute in der Geschichte**, in referring to Dilthey's statement that every genius metaphysician expresses through concepts a so far unnoticed aspect of reality, asserts that Schelling's genius consists in this "that all knowledge presupposes this last identity between thought and being," **loc.cit.**, p.43.

88. Cf. note 26, above.

89. **My own life**. Here quoted from Norman Kemp Smith's edition of Hume's **Dialogues Concerning Natural Religion**, (which includes Hume's autobiography), p.237.

90. **Op.cit.**, p.238.

91. **Op.cit.**, p.239.

92. **Op.cit.**, p.239f.

93. **Op.cit.**, p.76f.

94. **Op.cit.**, p.239.

95. August 16, 1783. Quoted from **Kant's Philosophical Correspondence 1759-1799**. Edited by Arnulf Zweig, **Op.cit.**, p.105f.

96. That part of the correspondence between Fichte and Schelling which shows how their relationship gradually aggravated, is reprinted in Walter Kaufmann's earlier mentioned book, p.124-129.

97. Translated into English by Peter Heath and John Lachs.

98. October 13, 1806. Here quoted from Franz Wiedmann **Hegel. An Illustrated Biography**. Translated from German by Joachim Neugroschel, 1968.

99. **Über Mythen, historische Sagen und Philopheme der alten Welt.**

100. Quoted from Walter Kaufmann, **op.cit.**, p.355.

101. Wiedmann, **op.cit.**, p.113.

102. About the ontological argument for God's existence, Schelling says: "There, however, is a difference between saying: God can exist only by necessity, or saying: He necessarily exists. From the former statement (He can exist only by necessity) follows only: therefore he exists by necessity; that is if he exists; it does not follow at all **that** he exists." **Zur Geschichte der Neuern Philosphie. Werke** V, p.15.

103. The title does not lend itself to an adequate translation. A person to whom the title is bestowed is thereby given a certain social status.

104. Wiedmann, **op.cit.**, p.11.

105. Wiedmann, **op.cit.**, p.19.

106. Karl Rosenkranz **G.W.F.Hegels Leben**. Here quoted from Wiedmann, **op.cit.**, p.97.

107. Here quoted from Walter Kaufmann, **op.cit.**, p.299.

108. Here quoted from **Nietzche** by Karl Jaspers. Translated by Charles F. Wallroff and Frederick J. Smitz, p.399.

*   [Since the ms preparation was assisted by Dr. Else Mogensen, Lars Aagaard-Mogensen, and the Philosophy Department

equipment of the Science & Humanities Division of RIT, Professor Justus Hartnack is of course not responsible for such errors as may be due thereto.]

INDEX

-------- A --------

Absolute (the)   40, 61, 67-71, 76, 78-82, 89, 96, 99, 102, 187
Absolute (or German) Idealism   2, 5-8, 21, 32, 169
An sich   99, 108, 111, 117, 141
And und fur sich   99
Apperception, transcendental (or Unity of Consciousness)
    23-32, 40-51
Aristotle   1, 15, 67, 89, 143
Art   60, 68, 72, 74, 81f
Aufgehoben   107, 160

-------- B --------

Becker, Werner   154, 206, 207
Berkely   155
Behaviourism   170

-------- C --------

Carnap, Rudolf   203
Cogito ergo sum   46
Concrete Universal   104

-------- D --------

Darwinism   186
Dass-sein   188f
Davies, Paul   201
Democritus   91, 92, 123
Descartes   15, 46f, 77, 78, 90, 117, 120, 153, 154
Dilthey   207
Dogmatism   36-39, 68
Dualism   5, 32, 56, 65, 68, 77, 86, 137, 153

-------- F --------

Fichte   5, 35-65, 67, 68, 71, 73, 75, 76, 78, 80, 81, 82, 83, 84, 89,
    90, 99, 105, 106, 156, 171
Findlay, J.N.   149, 151, 166, 170
Fink, Eugen   206
Freedom   37ff, 65, 69-71, 105
Fur sich   108, 111, 117, 141

-------- G --------

Glockner, Hermann   92

-------- H --------

Habermas, Jurgen   121
Hampshire, Stuart   197
Hartmann, Nicolai   121, 203
Hegel   2, 5, 6, 32, 35, 76, 83, 88, 89-166, 171
Henrich, Dieter   203
Heraclitus   1, 16
Hobbes   77
Hume   1, 2, 3, 4, 6, 8, 11-22, 28f, 32, 45, 84, 109, 110, 155, 168,
    169, 197
Hyppolite, Jean   204

-------- I --------

I (or the Ego)   3, 7, 16-21, 24f, 38, 40-64, 68, 71-74, 80, 81, 83, 87,
    102, 105, 116, 155, 157, 159, 168
Idealism   36-40, 68, 75, 76, 92
Intellectual Intuition   68, 80, 81
International Object   18
Intention   81
Inverted World   138

-------- J --------

Jacobi, F.H.   30, 35f

-------- K --------

Kant   2, 4, 5, 8, 18, 21-33, 35ff, 46, 67, 80, 84, 85, 89, 90, 93, 106,
   117, 120, 123, 124, 149, 151, 154, 168, 169, 171, 172, 197
Kasper, Walter   207
Kaufmann, Walter   149, 201, 208
Kojeve Alexandre   149, 150, 151, 205
Kroner, Richard   200, 205

------- L --------

Language - criterion   168
Leibniz   67, 89
Locke   17f, 90, 117, 120, 123, 124
Logical Positivists (their theory of meaning)   168, 169

-------- M ------

Maimon, Salomon   198
Malcolm, Norman   203
Marcuse, Herbert   165, 166, 202
Marx, Werner   198f, 206
Meta-language   6, 52, 171
Miller, A.V.   202, 205
Moore G.E.   203
Mure, G.R.G.   201

-------- N --------

Naive-realism   90
Negative philosophy   188
Negativity   101f, 114, 131, 139
Newton   77
Non-I (or Non-ego)   7, 8, 39, 40-64, 76, 86
Nothingness   47
Non-linguistic reality   21, 32, 53f, 56, 73, 85, 86, 87
Nietzsche   208

-------- O --------

Object-language 52
Ontological argument 188f
Ordinary language 118f
Olshenwsky 199

-------- P --------

Parmenides 1
Personal identity 17, 24
Plato 1, 45, 67, 89, 107
Positing 43, 48-51, 59, 60-62, 64, 72f, 75
Positive Philosophy 188
Potencies 186
Pre-Socraties 67

-------- Q --------

Quantum theory 91

-------- R --------

Radical empiricism 1f, 8, 11-20, 21, 169
Reinhold, Karl Leonhard 35
Res Cogitans 46, 77
Rescher, Nicholas 199
Rosen, Stanley 205
Rosenkranz, Karl 208
Russell, Bertrand 18, 117

-------- S --------

Schelling 5, 35, 67-88, 90, 92, 96, 99, 101, 105, 107, 171, 172
Scepticism 160, 162
Schulze, Gottlob Ernst (Anesidemus) 35
Specious present 26
Spinoza 67, 89

Strawson, P.F.   50, 199, 202
Stoicism   160, 161
Substance (category of)   24
Supersensible world   137

-------- T --------

Teleological explanations   63, 75, 78
Thing in itself (the)   4, 8, 21, 29-33, 35-38, 45, 67, 68, 80,
   82, 84, 85, 138, 172
Thing-language   118
Transcendental argument   20
Transcendental deduction   20, 31

-------- U --------

Unconditioned (the)   61, 67, 68-71

-------- V --------

Verkehrte Welt, see Inverted World
Via negation   128

-------- W --------

Wahl, Jean   163
Was-sein   188f
Wiedemann, Franz   208
Windelband, Wilhelm   166
Wittgenstein   81, 111, 197
World Spirit   102, 103

STUDIES IN THE HISTORY OF PHILOSOPHY

1. Justus Hartnack, **From Radical Empiricism to Absolute Idealism**

2. Leonard A. Kennedy, **Peter of Ailly and the Harvest of Fourteenth Century Philosophy**